W9-AMZ-660

COOL POOLS
AND HOT TUBS

COOL POOLS AND HOT TUBS

VINNY LEE

SPECIAL PHOTOGRAPHY BY **RAY MAIN**

Watson-Guptill Publications / New York

To AWJ—my companion in life's bubbly (hot) tub

First published in the United States in 2006 by
Watson-Guptill Publications,
a division of VNU Business Media, Inc.,
770 Broadway, New York, New York 10003
www.wgpub.com

Conceived and produced by Jacqui Small LLP, an imprint of
Aurum Press Limited
25 Bedford Avenue
London WC1B 3AT

Publisher Jacqui Small
Editorial Manager Kate John
Designer Ashley Western
Editor Sian Parkhouse
Picture Researcher Emily Hedges
Production Peter Colley

Library of Congress cataloging information in progress

ISBN 0-8230-0682-4

Manufactured in China

1 2 3 4 5 6 7 / 09 08 07 06

contents

POOLS COM

ME OF AGE

THIS PAGE Irregular-shaped boulders create a link between the pool and its surroundings and nominally define the shallower tub end from the main swimming area.

OPPOSITE The plain, pale stone of the pool surround echoes the soft hues of the materials used in the construction of this Mediterranean house. The dark-colored lining of the pool helps it to blend, rather than contrast, with the landscape and planting.

Whether in ponds, streams, the ocean, or purpose-built pools, the pleasures of water and the joys of swimming have been appreciated for centuries. Heated pools were built by the Romans in 50 BC, but the modern public pool didn't become prevalent until the 1800s. By the 1900s swimming was widely popular after its inclusion in the Olympic Games of 1896.

For many years, private swimming pools were thought of as a luxury, with connotations of Hollywood glamour, decadence, and even seduction. There were overtones of Dustin Hoffman in the movie *The Graduate* lying on his back in the water staring at the sky, of shimmering Hockney-blue rectangles, or even the grandeur of a Busby Berkeley spectacular with sequined swimsuits and synchronized swimming routines. But those days are long gone and the pool has now come of age—not only is it more widely available and less expensive to install and maintain than it has ever been, but the advantages of swimming in regard to physical and mental well-being have also come to the fore.

Swimming pools, spas, hot tubs, and Jacuzzis are now more than a summer indulgence. They have year-round appeal, and with full twelve-month use, the initial investment and overall costs are spread wider and therefore work out to be better value. The advances in pool design and technology, which have also been instrumental in bringing costs down, have increased the choice of size, shape, and construction available. You can now have a pool in the uneven and irregular contours of a rocky landscape or within the limitations of an urban yard. Smaller jet pools and hot tubs can be installed in restricted or redundant spaces such as cellars, roof tops, garages, or an outdoor building and even in a raised deck.

These smaller water-related tubs and facilities are increasingly popular, and this is put down to the fact that people perceive they are living pressured lives and look for ways to unwind, indulge, and reward themselves. The hot tub and similar spa equipment need only a small amount of space and are simple to maintain, but they provide physical and mental relaxation as well as a cleansing and health-restoring wind down at the end of a hectic day.

PERSONAL BENEFITS

Water has long been associated with spiritual and physical cleansing. Its buoyancy takes the weight away from the body, allowing it to float, defying the pull and pressure of gravity, for an

almost surreal experience. The cushioning effect of water can be enjoyed by simply relaxing back and floating on the water or lying on an inflatable mattress.

Water has many spiritual and remedial properties, and numerous religions encourage followers to use it as part of a ceremony. For example, in Christianity John the Baptist used submersion in water to initiate followers. Ritual purification with water is an important part of the Hindu faith, and among the most holy of its places are the bathing ghats on the River Ganges. Muslims ritually cleanse themselves before entering a mosque for worship, and many courtyards outside these holy buildings contain a fountain or pool for this very purpose.

In Zen philosophy running water is said to carry the force of Chi, which brings positive energy and well-being, and water is also recommended as an aid to meditation. The Tao philosopher Lao Tsu said, "Water is good for all living things. It flows without thinking where it is going." You don't have to submerge yourself in water; just sitting by and contemplating it can be beneficial.

Even without following these religions or philosophies, it isn't hard to appreciate water's refreshing and exhilarating effects. Think of a shower of water pouring over you and washing away the stress and anxiety of the day; or the smooth pressure of parting water as you swim through it; the sudden rush that forces past you as you dive into a pool; or the relaxing massage of warm, bubbling water jets in a hot tub or Jacuzzi: all these different types of contact with water bring both physical and metal benefits.

In addition to the spiritual and physically relaxing and reviving affects of water, it is also the ideal medium in which to exercise. The buoyancy of water counteracts the pressure of gravity, taking the stress and strain off joints, so running in water has less impact on knees, shins, and ankles than undertaking the same exercise on a track or treadmill. The exercise is further enhanced and made more effective because as you run or swim, you push against the water, which in effect is like working against a weight in the gym.

Swimming is widely regarded as the most effective full-body, low-impact exercise. It also has aerobic benefits, increasing heart

OPPOSITE This deep-lipped oval window at the home of the designer Pierre Cardin was created to frame the view. Its location and size means that the varying blues of the pool, sea, and sky are equally divided into three sections.

THIS PAGE Pools with infinity edges seem to disappear into the landscape rather than form a hard edge. Here the reflection of the surrounding trees further enhances the feeling of the pool being part of the grounds.

THIS PAGE A pool is more than just a place for a daytime dip; it can be part of a lighting plan that reflects light into the house as well as being highlighted as a feature in its own right.

rate and lung capacity as well as regulating breathing, which can be helpful for people with asthma and breathing-related problems.

The other feel-good factor that results from a good swim or workout in water is the release of endorphins, a natural substance produced by the body's pituitary gland and the hypothalamus. Endorphins not only regulate pain and hunger, but also produce a feeling of well-being. As the naturally occurring secretions disperse slowly in the body, this means that the beneficial effects are long lasting. The result is that you feel better on two levels, the first because you have exercised your body and the second because your general sense of well-being is enhanced.

A POOL OF YOUR OWN

Although public baths and pools have been in common use since Roman and Greek times, and were regarded as social forums as well as places to wash and exercise, the modern pool has become a more intimate, private place for family and invited guests.

There are many advantages to having a pool of your own, not least that you don't need to travel to use it, there are no lines, and you don't have to jostle with crowds, fight over lanes, or dodge divers. Your own pool will be a familiar place, one that you are comfortable in; you can use it for ten minutes or an hour and fit its use in around your timetable rather than the sports center's or health club's opening hours. The water temperature and environment can be set to your liking and the adjacent facilities, such as the shower and changing area, stocked with your lotions, potions, towels, and clothes. You don't have to pack a kit bag and carry it somewhere, only to arrive and find that you have forgotten your goggles, nose clip, or swimming trunks, or wrap up dripping swimwear and carry it home.

FOR FRIENDS AND FAMILY

Although a pool is a great place to be on your own or to follow an organized exercise program, it is also an enjoyable place to share. Just as a Turkish hammam or a Finnish sauna is a place for social gathering and conversation, so is a privately owned poolside or hot tub. As a meeting place for friends and family, a pool can be a focal point for swimming parties, games such as water polo or volleyball, or races and galas.

For a family with young children a pool at home is an ideal place to build up a child's confidence and proficiency in the water, as well as to respect it as a place of danger where accidents can occur. For people with specials needs or injuries, or for older members of the family, a pool at home will be a place where gentle and thorough exercise can take place in both privacy and comfort.

The pool or hot tub can also be a place where children and adults spend time together. In these days of juggling working and family life, making time to swim together or relax among the gently massaging jets of a hot tub can be valuable and constructive, a time to catch up with each other and the day's events.

POOLS FOR NOW AND THE FUTURE

Technological advancements, new systems of construction, and the increase in the number of private pools being built have seen a growth in the variety of style and types available. New materials, customer demands, and design trends have also been influential in the development and updating of pools and their surroundings. The prominence of the pool has increased, too. Its use is now more regular, and it is often accessed several times a day—in the morning, at lunchtime, and in the evening—not just for a single swim on the weekend, and it is frequently utilized throughout the year rather than just seasonally. This regular and sustained activity has also put an increased importance on the role and position of the pool within the home environment.

THE POOL ROOM

One of the most common developments in pool design is that it has become integral to a living space. No longer does a turquoise oblong stand starkly in complete contrast to its surroundings. Swimming pools and hot tubs are frequently included as part of an outdoor living room, an extension of the home, and a feature that complements the house or building to which it is adjacent. Pools are also being designed as part of the landscape, so that they are integral or sympathetic to the land on which they sit.

The outdoor pool room often includes a kitchen and comfortably upholstered sofas and armchairs, with a beach or extended pool rim for lounging in swimwear and sunbathing. This provides various levels or layers for the pool user to enjoy and also creates a break or barrier between the wet pool zone and the dry cooking, drinking, and shaded section. Indoor pools can also be part of a larger environment, adjacent to a spa, home gym, or exercise space, or a lounging, bar, and TV area (although all electrical equipment must be installed well away from contact with water). There are also in-and-out pools where doors can be opened to give access to a summer barbecue and patio area while retaining the option to be closed off for winter use. Glass-panel folding doors may also be double glazed and sealed for added insulation, but will still allow natural light through.

CHANGES IN SHAPE AND COLOR

Pool shapes and sizes have undergone a metamorphosis, with angular boxes being replaced by softer outlines. These organic shapes are more adaptable and can maximize the area available within the restricted environs of an urban patio or yard. Free-form designs can also work in an awkwardly shaped area. For example, in a small backyard with a long return at the side of the house, an L-shaped configuration can be installed. The L can combine a narrow but long section for lap swimming along the side of the house, with a shorter shallow section for family use.

Where the site width is a problem, there may be more scope for depth that could accommodate a small but deep plunge pool. The plunge pool can be made exercise efficient with the use of power jets against which one can swim—the power of the jets means that you swim without advancing, in effect swimming on the spot.

To complement the move toward organic shapes, there has been a shift to more natural colors for pool linings. More subtle shades of gray, green, and beige are being chosen because they blend into the landscape and are less harsh and jarring in interior settings. There is also a trend away from solid color—instead, new pools are being lined with tiles or tinted concrete finishes that have gradual shading or a mix of compatible colors creating a mottled or varied effect. One shade that is increasing in popularity as a single and dramatic backdrop is black. A black lining creates a mirrorlike backing that clearly reflects the sky above. Indoors, a black-lined pool will appear to be deeper, almost infinitely so.

There is also an increase in the use of natural materials to line pools, for example, embedded rounded pebbles or flat panels of slate and stone. These are suited to outdoor locations and can be used to integrate the pool into its landscape.

ECO ELEMENTS

There is much interest in environmentally friendly pools, not just in coloring and appearance, but also in content. Natural "pond" pools have had a strong following in Germany and Austria but are now spreading globally. Natural swimming ponds consist of two areas: a shallow plant-filled section and a deeper swimming channel. Plants in the shallow section work as filters, cleaning and oxygenating the water, which chemicals might otherwise be used to do. A pump keeps the water circulating and aerated, and a skimmer removes surface debris and dead leaf matter. Because these ponds tend to be shallower than standard swimming pools, and because of the activity of the plant life, the water is naturally warmer than a standard unheated cement-cast pool. The plants, reeds, and flowers at the pool edge not only look good but also attract a variety of butterflies and birds.

ULTRAMODERN

Although poured concrete is the most commonly used material for pools, there are innovative designs that use more unusual materials. The development of the glass pool has been making rapid advancements; using bonded reinforced plate glass, a regular shape can be devised. But the glass and bonding have to be strong enough to withstand the pressure and weight of the water. At a beachfront hotel in Durban, South Africa, the rooftop swimming pool has a glass-box section that is cantilevered out over the side of the building, giving the user an unearthly feeling of being suspended in midair as he or she swims.

With improvements in finishes and coatings, steel pools are also making their mark. The steel moves slightly with the variation in temperature, contracting when cold and expanding when warm, but a backing of soft insulation material accommodates this flexing. The insulation layer can also incorporate a heating mechanism so that the metal is warmed, therefore contributing to the water temperature for cool-weather use. The temperature control can also be reversed so that the steel is cooled, which in turn will reduce the temperature of the water on a hot day.

RIGHT Water can increase the perspective and view beyond a room. Here the area outside the open doors will appear bigger because of the shimmering water, whereas if the ground was covered with plain tiles or grass, it would be seen as a dense and definable mass.

LOCATING Y

OUR POOL

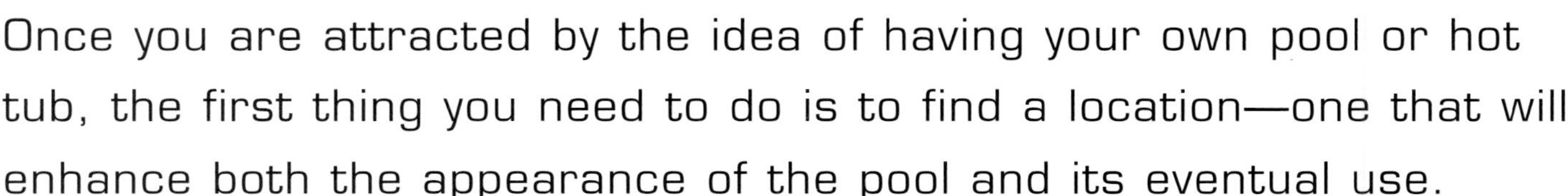

Once you are attracted by the idea of having your own pool or hot tub, the first thing you need to do is to find a location—one that will enhance both the appearance of the pool and its eventual use.

If you live in an urban location, your options may be limited by the small amount of outdoor space available, so you will need to create a pool that maximizes what space there is. For example, if you live in an apartment building and only have a terrace to work with, think of a jet pool or hot tub, and consider a lid or cover that will allow the pool or tub to become an integral part of the deck or terrace, or to be used as a table or lounging area when not in use.

A flat roof area, basement, or garage might also be used to house a pool and tub. The location may not initially seem very promising, but even the most basic structure can be strengthened,

insulated, and decorated to provide an attractive setting for a pool. Another option is to install a pool that is situated part indoors and part outdoors, making it a facility that can be enjoyed all year round and one that does not monopolize either the house or the yard.

Outdoor pools can be sited near a house and designed to complement its period and architectural style, as well as being an asset as a water and lighting feature. Alternatively, pool and tub areas can be styled to complement the outdoor environment, whether it be the immediate planting in nearby flowerbeds, the garden as a whole, or the landscape beyond, so it is a feature of a wider setting.

You might even be lucky enough to locate your pool in an area that allows users to enjoy a vista or view, overlooking a rocky coastline, endless acres of woodland, or a stunning city skyline.

INDOOR POOLS

Indoor pools come in many shapes and sizes, from the streamlined, linear lap pool used solely for exercise, to the colorfully decorated basement feature of Olympic proportions with lounging and entertaining areas and a play zone for all the family to enjoy. Pools in buildings will be either subterranean and windowless or at ground level or above and filled with natural light. The location will not only affect the quality and amount of light you will enjoy, but also the technical aspects such as ventilation, heating, and insulation. Indoor pools require more in-depth planning and involved construction and maintenance than outdoor pools, because the heat and moisture they generate can adversely affect the fabric of the building unless they are properly controlled. The weight of the water is another critical factor if the pool is located anywhere above gound level, and if a basement is excavated to contain the pool, then underpinning and additional structural support may be necessary.

The advantage of pools in or connected to a home is that they generally get more use. Protected from the weather and easily accessible, they can be enjoyed come rain or shine and be part of a whole exercise regime, or just a place for a quick dip and unwinding after work. Although some of the pool's surrounding walls may be of glass or mirror, the remaining ones can provide an area for color and decoration that will help to give style and identity to the space.

pools in annexes

There may already be an existing building adjacent to your home—an old garage, barn, or garden room—that could be converted or adapted to accommodate a swimming pool or hot tub. Exploratory work will have to be conducted to check whether there are any main drains, pipes, or electrical cables underground within the depth required to dig out for a sunken pool. If the pool is to be above ground, there will be a requirement only for a stretch of concrete or similar paving and adequate drainage and power for the pumps and filters.

If you are considering building a new extension to your home in order to house a pool, you may need to consult the building official's association in your state. Although it would not be classified as a residence, its size and volume may bring it within planner's restrictions. Although a pool house is most likely to be a single-story construction, you might consider adding a home gym or spa area on an upper or mezzanine level. If the main house and annex building are adjacent, it may be possible to knock through a doorway in the wall to connect the two directly. If not, an outside link under a covered walkway could be worth considering for ease of use.

The exterior style and appearance of the annex should be in keeping with that of the main building, but when it comes to decorating the interior—the pool and its surroundings—it can be a place to indulge in an exciting scheme. Because the pool is not an integral part of the main house, it can be treated as a separate unit and therefore more flamboyantly decorated. For example, a pool in a barn could pick up on the earthy woodiness of its surroundings and be lined with green rather than blue mosaics and feature teak and rattan furniture instead of chrome or plastic.

ABOVE LEFT This pool and Jacuzzi are part of a spa exercise area. The décor is clean and simple, making it suitable both for exercising and relaxing. Because the side wall is shared with the main building, the sources of natural light are from above, through a line of glass panels, and at one end via an external door and large windows.

ABOVE RIGHT The design of this pool utilizes the maximum floor space available in a converted barn. The original wooden structure of buildings such as this should be treated to prevent it from being affected by the constant moisture and heat given off by the pool water, and a high-quality ventilation system should also be installed.

OPPOSITE, TOP LEFT A stairway to the right of the pool gives direct access from this new-build annex into the main house. The annex features the same glass panels and angular style of the main building and benefits from abundant natural light through the wall of glass.

OPPOSITE, TOP RIGHT The boxlike pillars that are the structural supports for the pool annex are decorated as a feature and incorporate slimline lights. The gridlike style of the glass panel on the end wall emphasizes the geometric style of the overall design

OPPOSITE, BOTTOM The long graceful arch of a run of recessed skylights echoes the shape of the curving inset panels above the folding doors at the end of this annex. In a location such as this, side windows may not have been allowed because of the problem of overlooking a neighbor or an adjacent site, so natural light has been brought in through other, less obtrusive levels.

PREVIOUS PAGE This Scandinavian pool room has large expanses of glass, which help to make the indoor pool feel as through there is a close connection with the outdoors viewed beyond. The pool is small but adequate for a good aerobic workout.

cavernous splendor

Inspired by the dark, ancient mystery of natural grottoes and caves, the architectural firm Clarke Desai created an elemental pool in a suburban London garden building. Amenities and workings, such as a washroom, bar, and pumping and filter systems have been deliberately concealed behind oak panels and the slate walls and floors. This plan was devised to play up the natural grotto aspect of the building and to dispel any obvious links between the pool and the domestic aspects of the main house, therefore making it most definitely an outdoor room connected to the yard.

The pool is lined in gray-green slate, which extends out from the building into the small walled courtyard and garden beyond. The roof is propped up on large slate pillars, which are angled so that brief glimpses of the garden can be enjoyed from within the pool building. Artificially lit square panels in the ceiling give an illusion of natural light from above but can be dimmed and adjusted to suit the pool users' mood.

In spite of its elemental inspiration, the pool has a crisp modern edge, and a wall-mounted flat-screen TV is an unexpected feature, designed to alleviate the boredom of lap swimming for exercise and to celebrate the fact that this is a place created for enjoyment and indulgence as well as working out.

By focusing the design on a grotto and garden theme, the Clarke Desai team took the conscious step of breaking the link between house and pool, so that using the pool is part of a physical disconnection from home, domestic life, and its many distractions.

RIGHT Staggered floor-to-ceiling glass panels allow a clear view of the pool beyond but help to prevent heat and moisture from escaping from the immediate pool area. The large flat-screen TV, an unusual feature in such a setting, can also be viewed from the "dry" seating area on the near side of the glass.

LEFT Extra-wide supporting pillars are used to create a staggered screen that contributes a feeling of depth and perspective to the space.

ABOVE The angular sculptural steps allow wide access to the pool, making it easier for people to get in and out of the water at the same time. The steps are also deep enough to allow for sitting and relaxing at the water's edge before or after swimming.

OPPOSITE, TOP The flat-screen television has been set into the slate paneling of the wall. All the electrical wiring and the controls are kept well beyond the pool area for safety reasons.

OPPOSITE, BOTTOM Spotlights set in the ceiling create round pools of light on the floor that help to soften the predominantly angular design of the pool and its surrounding area.

Pool size
16ft (5m) wide by 26ft (8m) long by 6ft (2m) deep

Construction
The pool is constructed from reinforced concrete

What material was used on the ceiling?
Moisture-resistant plasterboard. The entire enclosure can be turned into a sauna or steam room at the flick of a switch

What tiles were used to finish the pool area?
Natural Welsh slate in varying degrees of smoothness, laid in random lengths

How is condensation dealt with?
There is a sophisticated ventilation and temperature, balancing system used in conjunction with heated glass throughout

Any acoustic work done?
A high-spec AV and lighting system was installed with surround sound and Lutron mood lighting

Heating system
Underfloor heating throughout

Filtration and cleaning
Ozone-friendly ultraviolet filtration

pools in limited areas

If you don't have an obvious space for a pool or hot tub in your home, try thinking outside the box, beyond the usual rectangle or regular shape. You may find that what a space lacks in width can be made up for in length, for example. With some investigation and research into what is available on the market and a little imagination, you may be surprised by what can be created in even the most restricted and unpromising of situations.

When both length and width are restricted, look into depth. A vertical plunge pool can be used for a refreshing dip as well as for active aerobic exercise—both the styles of pools and the use you make of them can be varied to suit the space available. For example, a jet pool, which is not much larger than a queen-sized bed, has an integral and adjustable water jet against which you can swim. This "swimming on the spot" can be as effective as a lap pool when it comes to exercising. The effervescent bubbling of a Jacuzzi can be a great substitute for a relaxing float in a larger location—the massaging and stimulating effect of the water will help to de-stress the whole body as well as direct specific jets of water onto a stiff neck or tense muscle.

Pools don't have to be angular; you can commission irregular or free-form shapes that fit into unlikely locations, such as under a staircase, or in a wide corridor subdivided so that the pool runs parallel to the main passageway, or even, with adequate structural reinforcement, on a spacious landing or gallery.

ABOVE LEFT Created in a narrow corridor, this lap pool has a graduated base and is accessed at the far end where there is a wider, open area. The round windows and well-positioned wall lights prevent it from feeling claustrophobic.

ABOVE RIGHT Combining angular and rounded shapes not only creates an interesting outline, it also maximizes the available space for the swimming area, and the rounded ends of the pool complement the ceiling arches of the architectural structure.

RIGHT A linear lap pool and an adjoining triangular tub have both been positioned within the confines of an awkwardly shaped basement. The use of the decorative fish motif panels and mosaics give the place an underwater dimension suited to its subterranean location.

OPPOSITE A Jacuzzi such as this could be installed in a cellar or basement. The bright decoration and well-placed lighting, both in and around the tub, give it a fresh appearance.

Pool size
8ft (2.5m) wide by 30ft (9m) long by 5ft (1.5m) deep

Construction
Poured concrete structure, fiberglass lining, and tiled finish, with 10mm mosaics at water level and 20mm mosaics below water level

What material was used on the ceiling?
Moisture-resistant plasterboard and underside of hardwood staircase with glass risers

How is condensation dealt with?
Air Handling Unit (AHU) provides reversible air-conditioning, creating hot and chilled air for ambient temperature, and introducing fresh air for dehumidification

Any acoustic work done?
Attenuation for AHU to both pool and gym areas, to mute the sound of the machinery; Barifoam lining; ductwork acoustically lined

Heating system
Heat reclaimed from compressor supplying power to AHU, heat directed into the water or air as required

Filtration and cleaning
High-rate sand filter and trace chlorine cleaning agent

pool and spa under the stairs

The proposal from the client to architects Paxton Locher and contractor Robin Ellis was to create a gym, changing area, spa, and pool space all in the same narrow room under the glass staircase off the entrance hall of a central London building. This request posed a temperature-control problem because a typical pool temperature is 68°F (20°C), whereas the gym temperature is 86°F (30°C). To solve the quandry, a separate gym air-conditioning unit was installed to blow chilled air in a vertical line between the gym and the pool, creating an air curtain that maintains the temperature differential within the overall space.

The original internal wall of the old building was retained, its arch and pillar formation giving the space character and interest. The glass stairs are opaque, so that the privacy of the gym is maintained while allowing light from the hallway to illuminate the pool, and the pool's reflection doubles the effect of the unusual architectural feature. The lap or lane pool's streamlined and architectural design shows how good use of light, space, and materials makes its pared-down no-nonsense style attractive and complementary to the location, although in a windowless space the pool feels neither gloomy, or restricted.

The linear pool is predominantly for exercise and is used in conjunction with a range of machines and equipment arranged in the gym area at the side. The pool's length makes it viable for lap swimming, but because it is open to the rest of the building and directly below the main entertaining and living rooms, the control of humidity and the use of low chlorine cleaners were a priority in order to avoid chemical aromas and dampness from affecting the upper rooms.

ABOVE LEFT Although the original arch features of the old brick wall have been maintained, the glass treads of the staircase give a light and contemporary feel to this restricted pool area.

OPPOSITE Lap or exercise pools don't have to be wide—an Olympic pool lane is 8ft (2.5m) wide, which is deemed adequate to accommodate a swimming stroke with outstretched arms.

indoor pools with a view

Water is an element that enhances other aspects of nature and a swimming pool, although a man-made feature, can be very effective in heightening the beauty of its surroundings. As part of an overall plan, a pool will act as a mirror, reflecting and doubling the impact of a forest or a mountain vista. Water will also add to the sense of tranquillity and well-being, bringing a feeling of calm and relaxation to a special place.

If the pool is located in a building with sliding glass door panels, the view will be more immediate, because with the lack of a visible barrier, it will appear to be close at hand. Also, when the outside temperature is pleasant, the panels can be pulled back and the fresh air and scents of the pines trees and woods or mountains can also be enjoyed from within the confines of the pool room.

Swimming in a pool in such a setting will have the added pleasure of making you feel that you are outdoors, without the discomfort of the change in temperatures the seasons bring. There is also a certain perverse thrill in swimming in a heated pool in an insulated room while looking out onto a snow-covered skyline or the dark clouds of a torrential rainstorm.

ABOVE Glass walls allow the bather to enjoy the surrounding woodlands, but the recessed pool itself does not interrupt the view.

RIGHT This round-edged pool contrasts with the hard rock of the view beyond while its tranquil surface acts like a mirror.

Pool size
6ft (1.8m) wide by 33ft (10m) long by 6½ft (2m) deep

Construction
Reinforced blocks with render

What tiles were used to line the pool?
Black mosaic was chosen so that when the surface of the water is still, it acts as a perfect mirror for the reflection of the surrounding trees

How is condensation dealt with?
By mechanical ventilation

Heating system
A heat exchanger is run off an oil-fired boiler

Filtration and cleaning
Sand filter with Blue Crystal purifying agents, selected for the low chemical use and their odorless aspect because the pool opens directly into the main house, so chlorine odor was not desirable

Dehumidifier
A Recotherme heat exchange system that changes the air 8 times a day, bringing in fresh and heating it with the heat recouped from the air being expelled

Special feature
The infinity edges create a false horizon, drawing the eye to the wooded countryside beyond to give the illusion of a natural stretch of water, in keeping with its location in a designated Site of Outstanding Natural Beauty

OPPOSITE The infinity pool stretches out into the woodland and mirrors the seasonally changing landscape around it.

RIGHT The pool is housed in a wing off a corridor from the main house so that the views on three sides are uninterrupted.

BELOW This view from the end of the pool looks back to the double doors that give access to the house, shower, and changing room beyond.

pool in the woods

This pool with a view, set on a wooded hillside in the Oxfordshire countryside, was part of a new-build project designed by architect Niall Mclaughlin. The plan from the outset was to construct a simple and inexpensive house with plenty of transparency so that a portion of the budget could be spent on an indoor heated pool.

The building is formed on a steel frame with Douglas fir timber paneling. Because the site is a designated Site of Outstanding Natural Beauty, the planning permit included a clause stating that no mature trees could be disturbed, so the building was designed to fit into the existing landscape and the house and pool stand like suspended boxes with only steel columns disturbing the woodland floor.

The pool is tiled in black to enhance its ability to reflect surrounding trees. When the owner dives in, he says he feels as though he swims straight out into the view. The glass walls and infinity edges of the pool help blur the line between indoors and out, and the mirroring effect of the glass makes it even more uncertain where one begins and the other ends.

basement pools

When considering locations for a pool in your home, think about basements and cellars—they are usually wasted spaces, used for storage and not much else. These dark and uninspiring locations can be made over into a pool complex that will give a whole new dimension both to your home and to your family activities.

Basements have a number of inherent problems that need to be addressed. They are invariably dark, may be damp, and often have low ceilings. To overcome the deficit of daylight, choose a white-based, bright color scheme with well-positioned artificial lighting, both in and around the pool. Sometimes it is possible to access some daylight by opening up an exterior stair- or light well. Damp can be contained with tanking membranes and special waterproof screeds. You may think that dampness should not be a problem in a room that is designed to hold water, but if uncontrolled it will damage the wall finishes and may encourage mold growth.

Low head height can be remedied by extra excavation; while the pool area is being dug out, a few extra cubic yards of soil can be removed from the surrounding horizontal surfaces so the new surrounding floor level is slightly below the old one.

In some metropolitan locations, pools have been created by excavating a section of a backyard, then building what is in effect a subterranean box, and finally re-laying the lawn or patio over the lid or roof of the box, so that the garden appears to be undisturbed but a new pool room lies beneath the grassy surface.

ABOVE This design's cream tones add warmth and a glass panel in the arch at the base of the stairs allows whatever natural light does come down the stairwell to penetrate through to the pool.

LEFT Mirrors and opaque and etched glass panels can all be used to create the illusion of more light and space.

OPPOSITE, TOP LEFT In situations such as this, where the reception rooms (here, a dining room) are on an upper level, either to take advantage of a view or because the house is on a sloping site, the basement is an ideal pool location. This pool can be used in conjunction with the adjacent yard during summer, but closed off and heated in the winter.

OPPOSITE, TOP RIGHT By excavating and lowering one end of the yard, this pool gained two large areas of glass wall that bring ample daylight into the room.

OPPOSITE, BOTTOM Dramatic bands of black tiles and a frame around an oversized light create an impressive design and give an expansive feel.

underground luxury

The simple appearance of this new-build urban basement pool, designed by architects at Powell-Tuck Associates, conceals the complex and high-quality detailing that has gone into its design, construction, and finish. The pool, which is easily accessible from the main house, is part of a subterranean "after hours" space, including changing and shower rooms and an adjacent media room. All the walls and the ceilings of the basement complex are reinforced to support the weight of the two-story house above.

Basements can feel a little claustrophobic, but the pale blue glass mosaic lining of the pool, combined with subtle optic lighting and the natural light that comes in through the glass walls from the stairwell

ABOVE A sculpted wooden bench butts up to an opaque glass shower screen in the dressing room beside the pool.

RIGHT Stairs beyond the glass wall on the left of the pool lead directly up to the main house above for ease of access.

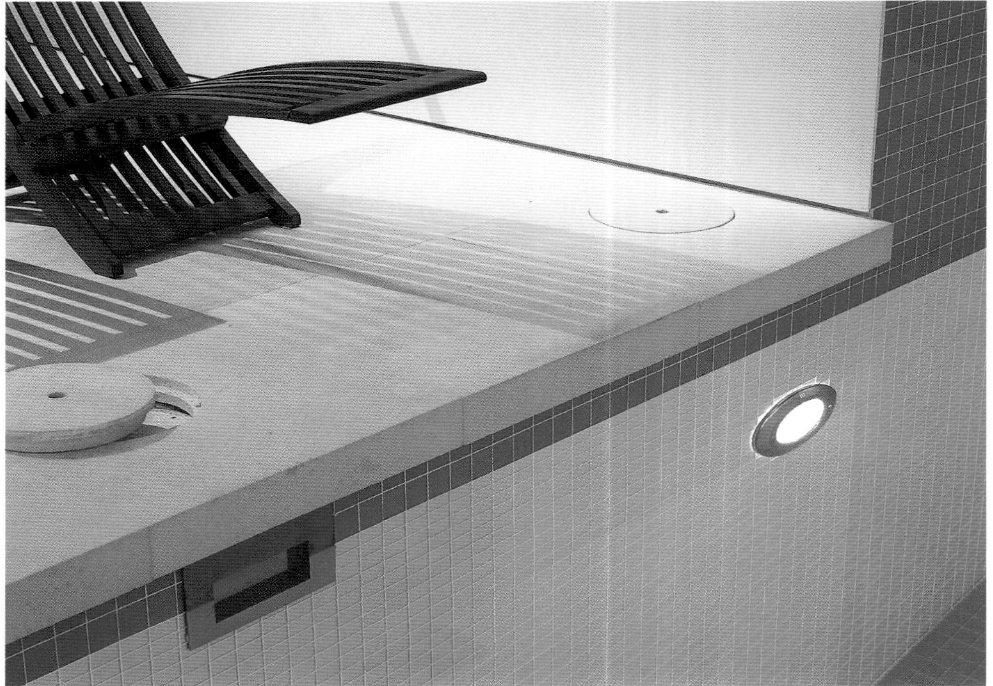

Pool size
15ft (4.5m) wide by 48ft (14.5m) long by a minimum of 3¼ft 3in (1m) graduating to a maximum of 6½ft (2m) deep

Construction
Reinforced concrete with waterproof render

What material was used on the ceiling?
Western red cedar

What tiles were used to line the pool?
"Atlantic" colored glass tiles by Reed Harris

Any reason for the shallow step access?
It looks good!

How is condensation dealt with?
Mechanical ventilation—fresh-air supply and extraction with dehumidifier

Any acoustic work done?
All ductwork was acoustically lagged

Heating system
A 6½ by 3¼ by 6½ft (2m by 1m by 2m) Calorex Delta 4 boiler and heat exchange unit in an adjacent plant room—the system heats and cools the air and heats the water (installed by E+M Technica)

Filtration and cleaning
Low-level, noninvasive subchemical system by Buckingham Pools

Special feature
The fiberoptic lighting over the pool area does not require access for maintenance

and a roof light at the end of the pool, all work in together to create a bright, fresh atmosphere that prevents this underground room from feeling boxed in.

The walls above the water surface are finished in off-white, riven-textured Portuguese limestone that, in its polished form, is continued on the pool surround as well as the hall flooring and stairs beyond. By using the same floor for the pool surround and the hallway, there appears to be no distinct division between the two areas, and all these pale surfaces reflect daylight into the pool area.

Wide, shallow steps allow easy access to the water for anyone using the pool, and the use of cedar wood paneling on the ceiling provides an earthy, natural element as well as helps to dampen sound, which might otherwise echo off the predominately hard surfaces.

OPPOSITE, TOP LEFT The round stone covers that slot into the pool surround conceal access to water filters, and sealed light units have been set into the tiled walls of the pool.

OPPOSITE, TOP RIGHT Below-water-level lighting makes the tile wall appear to be two different colors, although in reality it is all the same.

OPPOSITE, BOTTOM A long ceiling panel of reinforced glass allows daylight to come down from the yard above. It flows down the end wall of riven limestone, which looks like rippling water. The door at the far end of the pool gives access to the pump room.

ABOVE The natural light well at the shallow end of the pool, combined with light from the glass-sided stairwell, together supply ample illumination to this basement pool.

IN-AND-OUT POOLS

There is a growing interest in pools that physically span both indoors and out, allowing bathers to make the most of the refreshing water during warm weather and also continuing comfortable use at times when the temperature drops. But it isn't just the year-round use of indoor–outdoor pools that makes them so attractive; they can also have a secondary role as a dramatic water feature, visually linking the house to the yard. Even in an urban setting where the outdoors area may be limited, water may be used, instead of grass or paving slabs, as a ground cover. The water's moving, sparkling, and changeable appearance makes it a more interesting feature to look out on than static and solid stone, and the way the water reflects light and the color of the sky gives it endless seasonal variety.

The construction of the indoor–outdoor pool is much the same as a standard indoor pool, but the main differences occur in the maintenance and insulation. If your pool has heated water, you might want to incorporate a cover or sliding partition in the wall or floor so that when the weather is cold, the exterior sections can be isolated or cut off from the interior ones and only the water inside heated to body temperature. The water will also be subject to both internal and external debris and pollution, so a specially formulated cleaning process and high-level filtration system will also be necessary to cope with these demands.

partially covered

Pools partially set under a building can benefit from the shade or shadows created by the structure. There are times during the day, especially in midsummer, when the full glare and heat of the sun make it uncomfortable to be outdoors but in a section of a pool shielded by an overhanging balcony, terrace, or ceiling, the conditions for a cooling dip will be perfect.

Lighting in a pool connected to a building will be doubly effective at night. Light from within the pool will ripple and dance as the water moves, and wall-mounted or surrounding light will play off its surface. An indoor-outdoor pool can be illuminated with decorative lighting that becomes a feature when viewed from inside. The water will seem to extend the landscape, making even a small yard or terrace appear larger.

Sliding glass doors are often used to great effect over a split-location pool. The doors can be opened so that the whole room becomes part of the outdoor space, or closed so the water remains detached and a distinctive feature of the space beyond the screen. The inclusion or exclusion will change the character and ambience of the room, from an open and encompassing space to an enclosed and detached one.

The overhead covering section of a pool can also be louvered, perhaps with glass, metal, or wooden slats, so the light and ventilation can be partially or wholly obscured. Adjustable louvers are also useful in an open or exposed location because they are controllable—they can be altered when needed to follow the never-ceasing, diurnal movement of the sun.

OPPOSITE A timbered sun shield runs across the front of the house and also partially over the water, giving shade to both.

LEFT This overhanging roof construction shelters the pool, but leaves two sides open to the elements. An interesting grid on the underside contains lighting.

BELOW This elevated pool is set on a cantilevered balcony. The glass around the balcony and in the doors allows the view to be enjoyed from inside and out.

PREVIOUS PAGE A glass screen separates this outdoor kitchen from the lap pool that runs along the outside of the building.

half in half out

Designed as part of a whole new-build family home, this elegant north London pool was created by architects at Munkenbeck + Marshall for the all-year-round enjoyment of both adults and children. The pool is in a self-contained wing of the house, reached through sliding doors from the far end of the open-plan kitchen and family room. To the left on entry is a changing area with steam room and shower, all contained within a rounded wall faced with roughly hewn Muschelkalk stone. In contrast to this rough surface, the floor is

ABOVE The exterior deck area with the glass walls pulled back gives a full and open aspect to the whole pool room.

LEFT Door panels can be pulled over the water so the inner section of pool is isolated from the exterior for winter use.

OPPOSITE The full length of the pool when undivided is seen looking back in from outdoors.

LEFT By contrasting the smooth angular design of the pool with the rough-hewn, rounded wall of the changing area, the architects have given the design a more earthy and interesting appearance.

ABOVE In the changing room, the opaque glass shower door at the far end can be glimpsed in the mirror's reflection.

covered with smooth limestone and the pool and hot tub lined with mosaic tiles. The wood used for the exterior roof-level screen is iroko.

There are two distinct sitting areas, the one inside situated near a matte-steel bar unit, and the other outside on the deck area facing out toward the garden. The sliding glass panel doors can be used to cut off the interior, or to open it out into one large room spanning indoors and out.

The glass doors also extend over the pool and a neat automatic cover system, recessed in the floor of the pool directly beneath the door, can be activated to separate the inner and outer parts, therefore maintaining the temperature of the heated water inside, while the outer water is enclosed, keeping it insulated and protected from falling leaves and other debris and the worst of winter weather.

Pool size
13ft (4m) wide by 60ft (18m) long by 4$\frac{1}{2}$ft (1.4m) deep

Construction
The pool is constructed from waterproof concrete

What tiles were used to finish the pool area and Jacuzzi?
1$\frac{1}{4}$in (25mm) glass mosaic

How is condensation dealt with?
The inside is air-conditioned, with grilles over and under the glass

Any acoustic work done?
The Barrisol stretcher fabric ceiling reduces reverberation

Heating system
Gas boilers with heat exchangers

Filtration and cleaning
A filter pressure vessel with interim distribution and collection pipe work

What system is used to activate the doors and covers?
They are electrically operated via switches in the pool area

ABOVE The indoor seating area by the pool and integral Jacuzzi is furnished with lightweight woven rattan furniture and cushions, with small side tables.

LEFT At one end, three steel spouts provide high-pressure water for massage, while the integral hot tub is set within the perimeter of the pool and accessed by the same steps.

RIGHT A clever system of two automatically controlled pool covers can be activated to divide the inner section of the pool from the outer, and the glass door slides across to the far wall to complete the separation.

RIGHT This arched cover has a removable central section, but the end covers can be left in place to act as a windbreak or to give a certain level of sound insulation.

BELOW, LEFT AND RIGHT These tapering or two-stage constructions provide neat-fitting coverage for most of the pool but have additional wider sections to allow poolside space for changing or relaxing after a swim.

sliding covers

Another option in the indoor–outdoor pool equation is the outdoor pool that can be enclosed. Toughened glass or high-specification plastic and plexiglass covers can be used to give a good standard of protection from cooler temperatures and from the problem of falling leaves clogging the water in the fall.

The main advantage these mobile covers have is that they are versatile: they can be closed, partially opened, fully pulled back, or removed to suit the weather conditions at any time. Some of the more sophisticated covers have glare-free glass, integral ventilation systems, and electrically operated sliding mechanisms that draw the panels back at the turn of a switch.

If you are considering building a brand-new outdoor pool, you can incorporate a sliding cover into the overall design and construction from the outset. However, if you already have a pool, these mobile covers can easily be installed to extend year-round use. They will also help reduce the cost of heating the water because they will reduce surface contact with cold air, as well as keep the existing warm air contained within them.

If your pool cover is made of a material other than toughened glass, make sure you use a cleaning agent recommended by the supplier, because certain cream and foam cleaners can scratch and cloud the surface of plastic finishes.

RIGHT This dome form has segments that can be pushed back and folded. The raised center section gives good head height over the middle, although there is only restricted standing area at the edges.

BELOW Lightweight and unobtrusive covers such as this one are ideal in a location where a clear view of the landscape or a glimpse of the garden is important.

OUTDOOR POOLS

With indoor pools you are invariably restricted by the size of the location and the constrictions of walls and boundaries, but with outdoor pools there is often greater scope to develop the pool and its surrounds because there is more available space. These pools can be created to complement or highlight the exterior features of the building that stands beside it or as a focal point among the shrubs and foliage of a cultivated garden. An outdoor pool can be positioned to take in the best aspect of a view or hidden away in a secluded wooden enclave. The location can be chosen to suit your temperament and outlook; or if the ideal site does not already exist in nature, it can be planted and manipulated so that it conforms to what you want.

Some outdoor pools will be designed to be at one with the environment, hewn into a craggy rock side and hemmed with boulders, for example, or filled with the salty water of the sea. Outdoor pools are more often organic in shape than indoor ones, which tend to be more regular and geometric in outline. The organic or free-form appearance is often chosen because it sits more comfortably with existing features of the landscape or mimics or echoes the contours of the ground. Hard, angular lines are rarely found in nature, so the more fluid and natural shapes are far more fitting in the great outdoors. Let the land- or cityscape inspire and guide you; the environment will give you ideas that you can draw from.

landscaped to buildings

A pool can be sited at the heart of a building, as it's often the case in Mediterranean or Eastern countries, where a water feature is often placed in a central courtyard as a cooling feature around which the living and entertaining rooms are constructed. In other locations the pool is to one side, often at the rear of a house, where it can be viewed as part of the garden or landscape while still maintaining a degree of privacy and seclusion.

In an urban location the site of the pool will depend on where space is available, whether on a rooftop or in a passageway or side of a building. But being an architectural feature, as well as an exercise and relaxation facility, it should be easily viewed, or at least glimpsed, from within the building, to maintain a connection.

If the pool is situated directly beside a building, the design could echo or incorporate features from its façade. For example, the angular aspects of a 1930s' Art Deco building could be replicated in the perimeter of its pool, or the colorful renders and paintwork of the villas of Miami could be incorporated into the decorative design of the pool lining and its surroundings.

If you would prefer an understated pool that will sit almost unnoticed against your building, always select a neutral color for the lining, something that tones in with the surroundings, such as pale gray to blend with rocks or concrete render, or a soft natural green to complement foliage and planting.

ABOVE LEFT A linear pool on the rooftop of this metropolitan apartment follows the narrow angular lines of the surrounding buildings. The dark color of the lining blends with the metallic and concrete tones.

ABOVE RIGHT This first-level pool is positioned so that it catches cooling breezes rather than being enclosed in the lower courtyard. The elevated position also gives bathers a clear view through the archway to the sea beyond.

OPPOSITE, TOP LEFT Groups of boulders and the surround of this pool pick up on the color of the adjacent house. The irregular shape of the rocks, which soften the line of the pool's edge, also gives it a simple and rustic appearance that further complements the style of the building.

OPPOSITE, TOP RIGHT Instead of a path or flowerbed, the owners of this house have placed a lap pool at the side of their home. It fits in neatly between the house and the neighboring wall, and the vivid color of the pool interior contrasts with the otherwise naturally toned colors of its immediate surroundings.

OPPOSITE, BOTTOM The rectilinear outline of this standard rectangular pool is interrupted by square planters holding palm trees. There is still adequate space for swimming, but the planters set into the pool create a more unusual shape, which is in keeping with the building at its side.

PREVIOUS PAGE Outdoor pools with an infinity edge will mirror the surrounding landscape through the seasons.

ABOVE This modern two-story house has been built in a narrow plot, and the pool echoes the same regular, geometric shape. The pool's length helps to exaggerate the stature of the house.

BELOW A rich blue lining gives this raised pool extra impact and acts as a cooling foil to the adjoining vivid orange panel.

THIS PAGE Although this pool is concealed from the house by a low wall, it is open at the other side so the view across the countryside can be appreciated both from within the pool and from the building above. The simple, uncomplicated shape is in harmony with the building.

Perhaps the ultimate way to landscape a swimming pool or hot tub to a building is to give it a direct physical link and site it on top of the building itself. In its associations with penthouse apartments, a rooftop pool has an undeniable suggestion of luxury, but in fact a pool or tub can in installed in relatively small spaces and if you live in a city location with no other outdoor space, this could be your only possible location. Flat rooftops are perfect, although a structural engineer should be always employed to check that the site is strong enough to withstand the weight of the volume of water you intend to put there. The calculations should also include the weight of the tub or pool construction and, if necessary, the concrete or flat base on which it will be erected.

Access to a water supply will be necessary, although hot tubs can be easily filled with a hose, and an available power supply will also have to be on hand to run heating and filtration systems. You may also want to factor shade into your plans. A rooftop is generally exposed and unprotected, so it will be subjected to the full strength of the sun during the day.

Putting a tub or pool on a rooftop may give you access to some stunning views, whether across a bustling city's skyline or over treetops and other buildings to water or parkland beyond. But with this sort of elevation, safety is a priority, so strong railings, walls, or reinforced glass panels around the perimeter of the location should be at the top of your planning list.

ABOVE LEFT Sandwiched neatly between two raised sections of white painted wall, this lap pool enjoys an uninterrupted view to the sea, yet the taller section of wall acts as a windbreak and gives privacy to the rooftop sunbathers and swimmers.

BOTTOM LEFT Raised on a stepped plinth, this penthouse hot tub provides a place to cool down and relax while occupying only a small section of the narrow terrace.

OPPOSITE, TOP Opaque reinforced glass panels were used as a protective screen around the edge of this rooftop pool area, so the view is only marginally reduced.

OPPOSITE, BOTTOM LEFT If there are no views to enjoy, make the protective screen into a decorative feature in its own right. Here, black ceramic tiles have a sinuous white pattern that reflects dramatically in the tranquil pool surface.

OPPOSITE, BOTTOM RIGHT Water from the rooftop pool tumbles in a cascade into a lower trough, from which it runs through a filtration system before returning to the pool.

urban rooftop tub

Pool size
5ft (1.5m) diameter and 4ft (1.2m) deep

Construction
Cedar wood with an integrated bench

Heating system
Integral heating system and pump, maintaining the water at a cool 78°F (26°C) in summer and a warm 100°F (38°C) in winter

Filtration and cleaning
A specific ozone purification system devised for use with a wooden tub, and a low-chemical formula to keep the water bacteria free. All the pump equipment is housed in a separate cube-shaped cedar skid pack

Special feature
Wooden tubs must be kept damp at all times—if they dry out, the wood might crack and leaks could appear

The client's contract with designer Michele Osborne was to create the "wow" factor on the restricted space of the terrace of his tenth-floor London apartment. Michele installed a classic raised hot tub that doubles as a water feature and echoes the waters of the River Thames flowing close by. She then selected grassy plants that would survive the windy and exposed conditions and require little maintenance—the various heights and colors of plants in containers are arranged around the base of the tub. The tub sits on a cedar deck, which complements its external paneling. The deck is edged by flat, black paddle stones, which in turn are framed by a band of blue stone. Whether looking out from the apartment to the deck or sitting in the hot tub and looking toward the metropolitan skyline, the tub and terrace have more that complied with the requirement for the "wow" factor.

ABOVE LEFT A tapering ladder gives easy access to the raised hot tub, which looks out over London's River Thames.

ABOVE RIGHT A "river" of flat stones is used as a border rim next to the decking.

OPPOSITE When not in use, the tub becomes a water feature, with the fronds of the grasses and wind-resistant plants in tubs hugging its rim.

central courtyard pool

Although the view is an important part of this terraced courtyard, the pool was created not just to take advantage of that, but also as an integral part of the house complex. Built in the 1950s on the slopes of Beverly Hills, the swimming pool was originally designed to be the central feature of the courtyard and to extend the lines from the wings of the buildings on each side. The white decking and coping follow through from the interior flooring and emphasize the indoor–outdoor nature of the space, and the pool itself appears almost to enter the house, its base end directly adjoining the central glass panels of the middle section of the interior.

Although designed and built in the 1950s, the area has a modern, minimalist feel, and when the current owners bought the place, they preserved that while undertaking extensive renovation work of both the pool and the building. Under the guidance of the architectual firm Marmol Radziner and Associates, the pool was updated with terrazzo coping around the rim, selected to integrate seamlessly with the surroundings, and the plasterwork lining was redone with more modern materials that were carefully chosen to match the original coloring of the swimming pool. Contemporary elements and materials may have been used to repair and update the buildings and features, but they have not spoiled or detracted from the original lines or appearance.

RIGHT The size and shape of the pool were designed to echo the lines and form of the buildings and to be an integral part of the terrace, which lies in the center of three sections of the house. All the rooms facing the pool have floor-to-ceiling glass doors so that the focus of the view from each place is the blue of the pool, with the Los Angeles skyline in the distance.

Water also has a cooling effect, and the many opening doors means that any breeze or air passing over the pool surface helps keep the interior of the building well ventilated and at an enjoyable temperature. The appearance of the water is also psychologically calming and meditative, in keeping with the minimal and uncluttered architectural style and furnishings of the house and pool surround. The feeling of tranquillity is present indoors and out.

Although there are two strips of grass, one at each side of the pool, the planting and landscaping is kept to a minimum with only the treetops giving a hint of vegetation, —this clean surrounding concentrates the eye on the pool area and then beyond to the skyline of the valley below.

Pool size
17ft (5.3m) wide by 28ft (8.5m) long by 6½ft (2m) deep

Construction
Concrete base with renovated white plaster lining

What material was used for the rim and water line?
Vidrotil tile by California Art Tile

Special feature
The pool is designed to appear as an additional room, an integral part of the overall building design

OPPOSITE Pristine white flooring runs seamlessly from inside the house through to the terrace. This and the sliding glass doors blend the indoor and outdoor spaces. Because there is no loose earth, sand, or pebbles, the immaculate flooring is comparatively easy to maintain.

LEFT Each room looks out on the pool and terrace. Even when someone is in bed, the changing color of the sky reflected in the pool acts like a weather report, indicating the conditions and expected temperature.

BELOW The area surrounding the pool is kept uncluttered; two simple angular benches break up the whiteness of the patio, and in the balcony recess two lounging bases and mattresses are discreetly arranged. Even within the house, in the area where the pool butts up to the glass, there is no furniture to break or interrupt the line of view.

provençal stone

At this stunning rural location in the Provençe region of southern France, the client asked landscape designer Anthony Paul for a simple pool and tub from which he could view his garden and also enjoy the wider landscape, including Mount Ventoux in the distance. The client also requested that the pool should look natural, like the local *bassins agricoles*, or farm troughs.

With this desecription Paul created a very simple and wholly recessed rectangular pool, but intersected one corner with a round hot tub, which sits like a column plinth at the edge. By interrupting the angular lines, the pool appears altogether less rigid and severe.

A dark, mossy green was chosen for the pool interior because it would be unobtrusive and more in keeping with the setting, which includes areas of woodland and rows of elegant cypress trees. The color also cools and contrasts with the rosy hue of the stone used in the construction of the house.

ABOVE The wooden rim around the hot tub creates a visual link with the sunbathing deck on the far side of the pool.

RIGHT The pool and tub blend in beautifully with the house.

Pool size
20ft (6m) wide by 40ft (12m) long by 6½ft (2m) graduating to 3¼ft (1m) deep

Construction
Steel and block construction with Balau wood decking that conceals the automatic pool cover and the balancing tank that controls the flow of water at the infinity edge

What tiles were used to line the pool?
Dark green Italian glass mosaic

Heating system
Normally unheated as temperatures in Provençe rise to 90°F (35°C) in the summer, but for cooler times of year there is a gas heater

Filtration and cleaning
The pool is cleaned by a sand filter, and the water is treated by an Ozinator

OPPOSITE, TOP Local stone has been used throughout the garden for paths and low walls, and this has been carried through for the pool surround and steps.

OPPOSITE, BOTTOM Lavender and rosemary are planted in expansive beds surrounding the pool and the tub so that their scents perfume the air.

RIGHT A stipulation was that the pool should make the most of the views, so it was oriented to enjoy the best aspects of the countryside and the mountain in the distance.

BELOW A round hot tub at one corner breaks the formality of the rectangular pool.

In keeping with the request for a design sympathetic to the vernacular style, the locally sourced lightly colored Pierre Bourgogne stone, also used for the paths and walls, was carried through for the pool steps and the outer casing of the hot tub. To enhance the view from the pool, the facing edge was designed with an infinity overflow, so that the water laps over the edge rather than butts up to a hard and visible line that would intrude on the view.

A raised, two-level wooden deck area was constructed to one side of the pool, and it is used as a sunbathing and cocktail terrace. The wood is a smoother and less heat-absorbent surface than stone, making it more comfortable to walk on with bare feet or to climb out onto after a swim.

The planting in the low-level beds around the pool is of mainly aromatic plants such as lavender and rosemary, which scent the early evening and morning air and add to the pleasure of swimming in and relaxing around the pool. These plants are also easy to maintain and can be clipped back to a low level so they don't interrupt the view. They are also resilient and will withstand the lower temperatures of winter months.

landscaped to grounds

Siting an outdoor pool in a garden requires careful planning, not only in the choice of suitable size and shape, but also to make it an asset rather than an eyesore. A well-designed pool should be an integral and attractive part of the landscape as a whole.

Whether starting from scratch with a virgin plot or trying to fit a pool into an existing garden, take time at the planning stage to consider some basic points. For example, what overall shape and style is the plot? Is it a meandering, informal place where a rounded or organic design would be suitable, or is it formal, with terraces or steps and better teamed with an angular pool?

Most importantly, study the path the sun takes over your proposed site; will trees or existing structures keep the pool in shade for most of the year? A little shade can often be a good thing, but a row of mature leafy trees could create so much shade that the water is constantly cold and the area feels gloomy. And will deciduous trees and spring blossom fill the pool with petals and leaves or worse still, insects and resin? Having these natural features close by might create a pretty scene, but they will seriously increase your cleaning requirements.

When it comes to choosing a color for the inside of a garden pool, in most cases it is best to avoid the popular vivid turquoise blue, which can be a glaring contrast to the greens and subtle colors of shrubs and flowers. Instead, look at natural stone linings, such as slate or marble, or dark blue, moss green, or even pale gray tiles and renders. These more subtle colors will blend far more easily with the natural surroundings.

OPPOSITE, TOP LEFT A border of pebbles and wooden decking softens the outline of the pool and helps to integrate it with its leafy surroundings.

OPPOSITE, TOP RIGHT Earth was excavated and moved from this hillside to create a level area on which the pool could be built. A low wall retains the bank of earth as well as provides wind protection for the pool.

OPPOSITE, BOTTOM LEFT The plants and trees around this pool offer a little shade, welcome in the hot months, but not so much that the pool is overshadowed or hemmed in.

OPPOSITE, BOTTOM RIGHT Within the shelter of an old walled garden, a simple and uncomplicated square pool, bordered by low box hedges in raised brick beds, is in perfect keeping with the period and graceful style of the setting.

ABOVE Being on a hillside, this pool is at ground level and filled in on one side while exposed on the other. Pools can be constructed to fit between levels or set into sloping banks.

RIGHT A classic rectangular pool, with steps and a water feature, suits the formality of this well-proportioned garden.

There is also the choice between a sunken or raised structure, with the pool either recessed into the ground or built up from it. The excavations for a recessed pool will leave surplus earth that could be recycled to make raised flowerbeds to create a sense of seclusion in the area. A pool built above the surface of the ground may double as a restful place to perch. If it is wide enough, the top of the pool's raised walls will double as seating and can be softened with narrow cushions.

Sculptures and water features can be useful in integrating a pool into a garden setting. The water feature (also see pages 124–5) is attractive in its own right, but will also double as a source of replenishing and aerating the pool's water supply. Statuary has long been an attraction in formal gardens, and set near a pool edge it can serve to connect the two.

If in doubt about how best to integrate your pool into your garden or what is most suitable when it comes to planting around its edges, consult a professional landscape gardener or garden designer who will be able to advise you.

ABOVE AND RIGHT Around many garden pools you find a stone path or rim; this divide helps to keep foliage, insects, and dirt clear of the water. There are two levels of planting around this pool: tall grasses to provide a barrier and protective shield around the water, and low-level groundcover. Arable grasses such as oats and two-rowed barley, which are green during the spring but will ripen into rich golden ears during the summer would be attractive in the high beds, and herbs such as chamomile and scented mayweed could be used to provide a lower level of vegetation close to the pool.

poolside planting

This above-ground pool was designed by architect Piet Boon to sit comfortably in the flat open grounds of a rural garden in Oostzaan in the Netherlands. Although the lines of the pool are angular, the soft planting in the surrounding beds, devised by garden designer Piet Oudolf, reduces its rectangular severity and mellows the solid black form. Another feature that subdues the outline is the infinity edge, which visually blurs the rim.

A purpose-built garden room in soft gray stone and slate that complements the dark color of the pool is used for changing, storage, and the pump and mechanical systems. A simple steel shower stands at the foot of the pool, partially screened by a low, freestanding wall. The building is in a traditional style, which sits comfortably with the surrounding garden, lawns, and borders, and Oudolf's block-planted perennials and diverse range of grasses bring texture and color to the pool perimeter.

Designed to be a year-round attraction, the pool also acts as a mirror reflecting the sky, and in winter, when the water is warm and the surrounding air is cool, a mist rises from the water surface, giving it a spectacular and surreal aspect. The wind passing through the long grasses also creates a soft rustling sound that adds an auditory dimension to the overall enjoyment of the place.

Pool size
13ft (4m) wide by 90ft (20m) long by 6ft (1.8m) deep

Construction
Black poured concrete

Heating system
A gas-powered system

Filtration and cleaning
Sand filter with ozone

Special feature
An overflowing water system does away with the noise of skimmers and other mechanical filters because the dirt floats away on the overflow; because the water is constantly moving, deposits don't rest on the bottom

Accessories
The simple steel shower is set behind a free-standing wall enclosure. A traditional wooden bench endorses the feel of the location; it is a classic piece of garden furniture rather than a lounge chair or other obviously poolside seat

Planting
The types of grasses you can plant in beds like these will depend on whether your soil is acidic or alkaline. New wave Dutch garden expert Piet Oudolf takes his inspiration from nature and integrates herbaceous plants, umbellifers, and grasses for a scheme that focuses on texture and color

OPPOSITE, BOTTOM LEFT The summer house and pool are seen in the context of the wider landscape. The planting echoes the pool's long angular shape.

OPPOSITE, BOTTOM RIGHT The shower is opposite the figure sculpture, in keeping with the symmetry of the whole layout.

LEFT The angular line of the rim is broken only by an amusing sculpture of a rolling figure.

ABOVE The beds of tall grasses screen the pool from a distance and give it a sense of enclosure.

RIGHT The only furniture around the perimeter of the pool is a traditional wooden bench.

part of the environment

This type of pool is set firmly in the landscape, not concealed or sheltered by the seclusion of gardens or flowerbed planting; it is a pool that is very much part of, and is exposed to, the great outdoors, and it will take inspiration for its appearance from the setting in which it is located. This type of pool is usually a much larger project than one ensconced in a domestic setting, not just in a physical sense, but also in the sheer scale of its dramatic effect on the wider landscape. This style of pool is a grand gesture, so it is very important to get the design absolutely right.

Most pools landscaped to the environment will be oriented to focus on a feature or outlook–a rocky outcrop of mountain, a lush forest canopy, a stretch of surf-filled coastline, or a particularly gnarled and twisted ancient tree. Whatever your chosen focal point, work backward from it and endeavor to create a pool that will sit comfortably within that landscape.

Infinity pools, where the water laps over the edges, making the outline appear to disappear, are often used in these locations. The water's edge can be positioned so that it seems to flow off to the horizon; therefore, there are no hard edges or definitive lines to disturb the panorama. This is particularly effective on sites that are set on hillsides. Another trick used to integrate a pool into a rocky or coastal setting is to interrupt the rim by placing a couple of large rocks or stone slabs over it, so that the monotony of the continuous, and therefore unnatural-seeming, line is broken.

ABOVE LEFT This pool's basic design is sympathetic to the rugged landscape, and the green interior complements the lushness of the shrubs.

ABOVE RIGHT In this cultivated environment the roundness of the pool sits comfortably with the rolling hills in the distance.

LEFT This pool wraps around the base of a rocky outcrop.

OPPOSITE, TOP A wide open space easily accommodates a rectangular pool, the simple and uncomplicated design of which suits the surroundings.

OPPOSITE, CENTER This pool appears to be a continuation of the sea; its infinity edge blurs the outline so the two appear to join.

OPPOSITE, BOTTOM LEFT In this Balinese location the wooden decking links the rain forest to the water's edge.

OPPOSITE, BOTTOM RIGHT The stepped shape of the surround and the shelving of the interior pick up on the ziggurat motif that is found in Eastern buildings and textile designs, and endorses the pool's Far Eastern location.

LEFT There is no natural shade around this exposed rooftop pool, so shelter is essential. An open-sided canopy with fine metal supports has been erected so the views can be enjoyed under protection.

OPPOSITE The pool's unusual shape is exaggerated by the double-lip edge; otherwise, the finish and color have been kept simple and understated.

sea, sky, and swimming

This rooftop pool in San Miguel, Ibiza, has been designed to make the most of the views across the bay; it was created as though recessed into the roof of the house so that there would be no obstructions or interruptions to the incredible vista. The exterior of the pool is built and finished in the same material as the house, and its shape follows the building's outline in a Z shape, with two larger cubes linked by a narrower center section. The base of the pool is graduated so the water is shallowest by the steps leading from the deck area and deepest at the outer edge. This is partly a safety feature, so that the bather is well submerged and mainly below the rim of the unprotected viewing side. This pool is effectively divided into sections, which can be a practical option for the demands of a family where a large, deep pool is set aside for serious swimming while a shallower, possibly stepped area is reserved for children or lounging rather than active water play. Even in a pool without a blue liner the water will appear blue, because of the volume of water and the reflection of the sky. In the deeper pool the tone or shade of blue will be darker, whereas in the shallower pool it will be lighter and more vibrant.

Pool size
The longest walls are 10ft (3m) and the shortest 6ft (1.8m) with the depth graduating from 6ft (1.8m) to 8ft (2.43m)

Construction
Concrete with fine white render on the pool's inner walls

Filtration and cleaning
Low ozone filters clean the water as it is circulated through the pool edge overflow

Drainage
Because the pool is on a rooftop there is comparatively little debris, occasional leaves and bugs are found but not as regularly as one would find in a garden level pool so pool edge mesh filters maintain the cleanliness of the water, and a manual net is used for any large leaves or petals

Special feature
The double-lip pool rim has three functions: it is a safety feature, the overspill of water visually softens the edge, and it catches and recycles water as part of the filtering system

THIS PAGE The pool is seen here in conjunction with the view at dusk. The rocks and boulders along the rim are arranged on a reinforced shelf.

OPPOSITE, LEFT The terrace area is finished with irregular stone paving, which picks up on the naturally asymmetrical and erratic rock formation and the organic shape of the pool.

OPPOSITE, RIGHT The rocky wooded surrounding landscape was the inspiration for the natural color, unusual shape, and stone rim of the pool.

Pool size
20ft (6m) wide by 40ft (12m) long by 10ft (3m) deep

Construction
Concrete with a fiberglass lining

Heating system
The pool is not heated

Filtration and cleaning
A "crawler" moving pipe sweeper on the pool bottom and a saline filter

Special feature
A reinforced rim to support the overlapping arrangement of rocks

hillside swimming pool

This pool was designed in an irregular, organic shape to blend in with the indigenous South African landscape and the surrounding rocky hillside into which it has been partially built. The pool has a reinforced shelf to support the rocks that overlap the rim, and they are part of its integration with the location.

The interior of the pool is finished with a charcoal-gray fiberglass lining that makes it appear deeper than the 10ft (3m) it really is. The dark gray coloring also looks more natural in the rocky landscape, but when the sky is clear, the water takes on a bluish hue from the sky's reflection.

The pool and adjacent terrace area have been laid out to make the most of the view out over the countryside to the ocean, and a series of submerged lights make it a year-round nighttime design feature. Integrated into the rocky terrain, the pool has no clearly defined edge on the far side so it appears to emanate from a source somewhere in the wooded landscape, and could perhaps be fed by a spring or river; this carefully planned design feature adds to the natural aspect of its rural appearance.

saltwater basin

Designed by its French owner as a "basin" for thalassic therapy, this seawater-filled pool on the coast of St. Barts in the Caribbean was inspired by Japanese, health-oriented bathing habits and the very simple tubs in which the Japanese bathe. The owner wanted the basin to be very natural and artisanal in its construction, in keeping with its holistic use and its coastal setting.

Every two days the pool is emptied and refilled with fresh seawater. A small electric pump carries out this operation, and once the pool is full, the water is allowed to settle for around two hours. Then, when the water is clear, it can be used for swimming or bathing. A minimum submersion of 15 minutes is recommended to enjoy the maximum benefits of the water's natural minerals and salts.

Pool size
Irregular, with a short wall of 13ft (4m), a long wall of 16ft (5m), and a depth of 8ft (2.5m)

Construction
Local rock bound with concrete

Heating system
The pool is heated only by the sun

Filtration and cleaning
Natural seawater

Water exchange
A small electrically operated pump to empty and fill with seawater

ABOVE LEFT Although a more recent addition, the seawater pool is part of an outdoor living arrangement; decks link the house to the lounging areas to the sea.

ABOVE RIGHT A series of stepped teak boardwalks provides ample and comfortable sitting and sunbathing space on the steep rock face.

OPPOSITE The pool is not only for thalassic bathing, it is also child friendly, with access via a series of small steps where children can sit and enjoy the surroundings.

USING YOU

R POOL

Having tackled the location and setting of a pool within the larger environment, this chapter is about the more immediate and personal use you make of a pool, as well as how you can customize and tailor it to suit your lifestyle. To get the best and most lasting pleasure from your pool, it is important that you feel comfortable there, both physically and aesthetically, and is somewhere you will enjoy spending time.

Design and decoration will play an important part in how you respond and react to the pool, as will the ambience and the physical environment, such as the temperature, and all of these factors need to be considered in combination. Your pool can be tailored to suit individual needs or those of family. It can be designed as part of an entertaining area, as a place to be enjoyed with young children or focused on exercise and fitness. It is your personal statement.

An increasingly popular type of outdoor pool that is very much a specific choice is the eco pond. The theory behind these garden water holes is that you create clean, safe water for swimming without the use of chemical purification, which appeals to anyone concerned about the environmental issues of constructing a pool, or indeed high operating costs. Aquatic plants and microorganisms contained in a perimeter section break down and absorb the nutrients that promote algae growth. The cleansed water is then skimmed and pumped back through to the central, unvegetated swimming zone.

Just as the eco pond drew on biotechnology in its development, other advancements are bringing pools into a new era, using not just the latest technology, but also different materials, such as steel and glass. The choice has never been greater.

FUNCTION AND USE

Although a pool may be an attractive feature in a backyard or even a selling point for a penthouse apartment, we should not forget that the main reason for having one is to be able to get into the water and swim on a regular basis, so while the color and design are significant, the way it is used and how it functions are equally so. Ease of access, safety, comfort, and practical aspects such as storage for cushions, games, and equipment all need to be taken into consideration, as do heat loss, condensation, and ventilation, the prices of which must be factored into the annual operating costs.

One of the most important factors in making it an area conducive to lingering and relaxing, as well as activity, is the temperature of the water and ambient air. Though of less concern in an outdoor pool, in an enclosed pool guidelines suggest that the water should be around 80°F (27°C) and the air 85–90°F (29–31°C). By keeping the pool surround at a slightly higher air temperature, you can help to limit heat loss and evaporation from the water's surface. Because of the ambient heat, some water will evaporate from the pool, and to keep the surrounding area from becoming humid and unpleasant, this excess water-heavy air should be mechanically removed. Typical indoor pool area humidity should be controlled at around 65 percent. If it is higher, it will not only make the environment feel uncomfortable, but if maintained at this level, it could damage the materials and infrastructure.

outdoor rooms

A swimming pool can be part of a whole outdoor living complex, a focus of activity around which there is an assorted arrangement of furniture, maybe a built-in barbecue or other cooking equipment, and changing and shower facilities. These additional resources will be centered on the pool, but they might make use of existing adjacent buildings, such as an old wood shed, or employ a temporary structure such as a canopy or awning.

Other locations may evolve gradually with use, rather than being planned from the outset. For example, a family that finds they are spending more and more time by the pool might facilitate their time there by laying in some conveniences. They might decide to build an extension as a permanent place to plug in a mini fridge or store furniture when it rains, and as a shelter from the sun or, at cooler times of the year, the wind, so that they can enjoy a prolonged period of the al fresco living they have come to like.

With a converted or new-build structure, electrical power cables can be brought to the site during the excavation works. This work should always be done by a professional since the cables need to be covered in strengthened insulation pipes and buried at a certain depth to meet safety requirements. In some locations solar power may be an option, because pools are usually situated in an open, sunny location, so a couple of solar panels in the roof of the adjacent pool house may provide the energy to run the pumps, filters, and other machines needed to maintain the pool.

If you decide to construct a simpler, more temporary structure for use in the summer months only, such as a canvas canopy, you should still consult an expert about using any electrical equipment, such as lighting. To run a small fridge, motorized spit, or barbecue

ABOVE LEFT An unused agricultural storeroom has been renovated and opened up to create an outdoor room with a hearth and built-in stone benches with cushions. The room looks directly out to the pool and is part of a year-round living space because the shelter of the building and its open fire mean that even on clear but chilly fall days there is enough protection and warmth to sit out comfortably.

ABOVE RIGHT Although sun can warm and invigorate, too much of it can be a bad thing, and at times we all need a little cool and shade. Here, under the protection of an overhanging screen, the view can be enjoyed at a comfortable temperature.

OPPOSITE, TOP LEFT The tall clipped hedges surrounding this pool give it a distinct roomlike feel. The hedge "walls" provide privacy and protection, therefore creating an intimate and personal space.

OPPOSITE, TOP RIGHT If building a poolhouse from scratch, locate it so that the structure provides shelter from the midday sun and prevailing winds. The building may also be oriented to provide privacy from neighboring houses. The front or face of the house should focus on the pool, and if left open, may benefit from breezes passing over the cooling surface of the water.

OPPOSITE, BOTTOM A pool house can be a place to indulge. If it is set away from the house, you can choose a different, more ornate style from that of the main building. Here, carved Indian pillars have been incorporated into an elegant year-round outdoor room.

PREVIOUS PAGE This pool surround is well planned, with areas of garden and patio, and places of shade and sunshine. There is also an outdoor shower and some comfortable furniture for both relaxing and sitting.

ABOVE Folding doors can be opened to make a room part of a larger outdoor living space. Here, folding doors give an open aspect to a kitchen dining area and make it easily accessible from outdoors.

BELOW This dramatic open-sided structure is furnished with lights, tables, and chairs, as in a conventional living room, and gives the impression that the adjacent pool is a rug or part of the general furnishings.

you could invest in a gas-powered generator for the site. Otherwise you can select portable equipment that has been specifically designed for camping use, and will therefore run on oil, kerosene, or butane gas, or is battery operated.

If your pool is situated close to the main house, part of it might also be transformed into an outdoor room during the summer, for example; where a pool is close to a patio and a set of glass sliding doors, the doors can be pulled back so the room becomes part of the pool and its surroundings. There is often a dry area, sometimes referred to as "the beach," between the house and the pool, which is a raised patio or deck on which furniture, chaise lounges and an umbrella can be arranged.

THIS PAGE A roof cantilevered from the side of the main house and under-filled with glass panels creates a single-story room with its main outlook on the water.

terrace living

Architect Bruno Erpicum was commissioned to design a pool for a client who swims every day and all year round, so it had to be practical to use and maintain but also attractive enough to take up a prominent position on a terrace with a stunning view and to complement the rectangular lines of the building it faces.

The swimmer using this pool can enjoy a 180°-degree view of the surrounding countryside and, when standing, the additional view of the landscape below. Behind the pool is a pillared colonnade, which fronts the house and provides a cool place of shelter away from the glare of the sun, as well as acts as a link between indoor and outdoor spaces. At night the reflection of the moon and stars on the water makes it feel as though "the sky is attached to the ground," and from both pool and terrace the array of twinkling evening lights below can be admired.

OPPOSITE, TOP The pool is part of an outdoor patio and adjacent enclosed living area. Sliding glass doors allow the living area to be opened up so that it, too, can be included in the outdoor space.

LEFT The size and shape of the pool were designed to complement the minimalist modern lines of the building it faces, and the finishes blend with its color scheme. Only a single, dark piece of sculpture breaks the clean lines and introduces a contrasting color.

OPPOSITE, BOTTOM The spectacular view can be enjoyed from both the terrace and from within the pool.

BELOW Deep sills on each side of the pool create a balcony, and the section of pool located between them has an infinity overflow, that removes any hard line or obstruction between the view and the observer.

Pool size
12½ft (3.8m) wide by 46ft (14m) long by 5ft 3 in (1.6m) deep

Construction
12in (30cm) reinforced concrete floor and walls

Any acoustic work done?
The facings and positioning of the surrounding walls and pillars have been arranged so that the noise of the water in the pool can be heard in the background, giving a fresh feeling to the whole patio area

Heating system
An automatic, electronically operated solar heating shutter is used to heat the water and to avoid evaporation. When not in use, the shutter rolls back into a recess

Filtration and cleaning
Sand filtration

family room

There is no age gap when it comes to pool use; the buoyancy of the water can be enjoyed by all, from a babe in arms to great grandparents. Water is a multipurpose forum, providing a versatile medium in which you can unwind and relax, play games, or take part in therapeutic aqua aerobics. As with all categories of swimming pool, safety is important, but even more so where the young, old, and inexperienced are at their most vulnerable. There must always be an adult available to supervise young children in and around water, and it is advisable to have a younger person on hand to help an older swimmer get in and out of the water.

When designing a pool for family use, focus your selection for the surround on nonslip surfaces, which come in a wide range of finishes. For an existing pool, runners of rubberized matting will be a worthwhile investment (see pages 146–8).

Although a pool can be an attractive backdrop for entertaining, it is unwise to mix alcohol and swimming. Hot tubs, saunas, and steam rooms can also be dangerous because they encourage the

ABOVE In an indoor pool room it is important to regulate the air flow, humidity, and temperature to make it a comfortable place for all ages to enjoy.

RIGHT Although the pool makes an attractive background to the bar, it is unwise to swim after drinking alcohol, but it can be enjoyable to unwind with a drink and friends after exercising.

OPPOSITE, LEFT A shallow or gently sloping pool rim is an ideal place for small children to play in the water while not getting out of their depth, but children should be supervised at all times by a competent adult swimmer.

OPPOSITE, TOP RIGHT Wooden decking is kinder to bare feet than stone and is also less hard if a child slips or falls on it. Pool sides can be decorated to make them family friendly and fun; here a large lighthouse acts as a beacon to the door of a changing room.

OPPOSITE, BOTTOM RIGHT The sides of the pool have wide stone paved edges with a row of pebbles that separates the wet pool rim from a sandy play area.

body to sweat and therefore loose fluids, which can intensify the effect of the alcohol and the dehydration it causes.

Efficient temperature, ventilation, and humidity control are imperative in an indoor family pool especially, because young and old members of the family will be prone to chills and exposure to temperature extremes. Creating the right atmosphere will not only increase your family's enjoyment of the pool, but will also help maintain its structural condition. The most effective and energy-efficient system is a heat pump dehumidifier, known as a HPD. This recirculates the air using a large fan, removes the excess moisture, and automatically reroutes it into heating the pool water while a controlled amount of fresh air is added continuously to maintain air quality. The system also operates in reverse so if the pool is too hot, the system will divert from warming to cooling.

entertainment center

This subterranean pool is part of a new-build family home designed by Alex Michaels of Michaels Boyd architects. The mandate was to create a childfriendly home for a family with three children. The basement pool, around which bedrooms and bathrooms are located, also acts as a source of natural light. A small, stepped rear recess allows light to shine through glass doors at the end of the pool and flow through surrounding walls of glass panels.

Safety considerations were a priority in the pool design. The depth is a constant 5ft (1.5m) so that it is comfortable for an adult to stand in the water and hold a child during a swimming lesson. The whole area is enclosed and can only be accessed by a programmed fingerprint recognition panel in the main door. There is also a semi-rigid, roll-over cover and wide, gently sloping steps, the latter providing a seat for parents to sit on while keeping an eye on the children, and also for safe and easy access.

But the pool complex is not only a child activity zone. The lights in the ceiling by the pool's long solid wall are multicolor rotation LEDs with a color and sequence adjuster by Modulor. These lights change color and, when linked with the music system, change with the beat. The beams play off the surface of the water and reflect, through the internal glass wall, off the white wall opposite, creating a moving color show that can be seen on the floor above.

THIS PAGE Glass walls make the pool a visible feature at the center of this home. Designed specifically for a family with three young children, it is enjoyed by the children during the day, while the adults make the most of it when their offspring are tucked in bed—but can still keep an eye on them through the glass walls that look out onto their bedroom doors.

OPPOSITE Games such as water polo are popular with children and adults alike.

Pool size
10ft (3m) wide by 23ft (7m) long by 5ft (1.5m) deep

Construction
Waterproof concrete

What tiles were used to line the pool?
Bizazza white glass mosaic

Heating system
Heat exchanger and pump that work off the borehole supply

Filtration and cleaning
Sand filtration and ozone with minimal chlorine

What type of ventilation system is installed?
Dehumidifier works off the heat pump (working off a borehole)

Special feature
The childproof door lock is a fingerprint recognition lock by Biomega that opens only when pressed by an adult whose fingerprint is programmed into the system

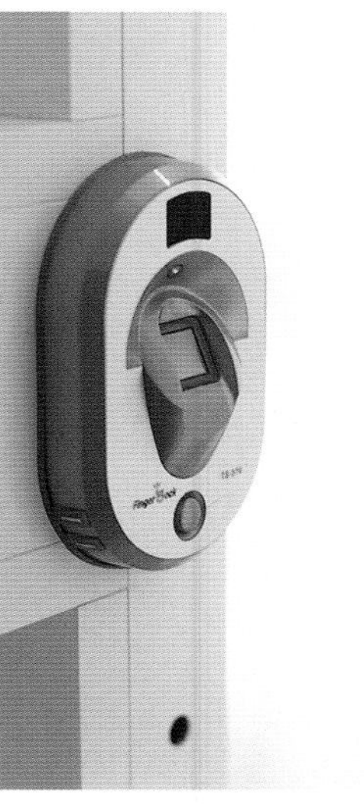

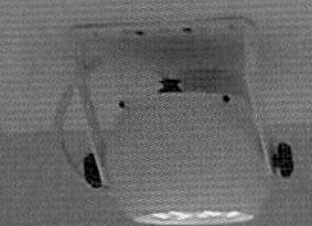

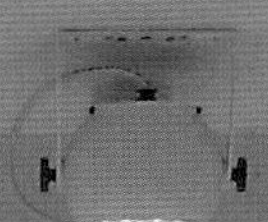

THIS PAGE Wide, shallow steps were designed for easy access and to give adults a comfortable perch while supervising children.

OPPOSITE, TOP RIGHT Built-in wooden lockers at the base of the internal glass walls store pool toys and sports equipment .

OPPOSITE, LEFT The stepped rear access to the pool allows daylight to illuminate the inner area, and the glass walls let it flow to the core of the house.

OPPOSITE, CENTER The door to the pool has a childproof fingerprint recognition lock.

OPPOSITE, BOTTOM RIGHT The multicolor rotation LEDs with sequence adjusters create a changing lighting effect that can be seen though the house.

exercise pools

Pools that are primarily for exercise are usually indoors so that they are operational throughout the year, and the pool is frequently used in conjunction with a gym area housing exercise machines or a spa and sauna annex. Glazed conservatory-type enclosures, extensions, glass sliding doors, and skylights help to create a light outdoor ambience, which is important in promoting a feeling of well-being but glass structures are prone to condensation, heat loss, and glare, so address these problems at the planning stage.

Glazing around a pool area should be at least double, but ideally triple, thickness, and internal doors and windows must be well sealed to prevent the damp air from seeping out and prevent cold air from coming in. In this enclosed environment with the unavoidable inherent moisture, there is an added increase in the problem of condensation. This occurs when the temperature is different on each side of the glass, but it can be remedied by installing warm-air vents at the top or base of the window or panel.

Although a wide pool can be useful if there are more than two swimmers exercising at a time, a linear or lap pool can be slotted into an area where a full-sized pool might not fit. In very confined spaces a jet pool can produce a strenuous workout. The jet pool's system creates a current against which the swimmer moves, so instead of the swimmer propelling him or herself through the water, the water acts as a force against which the swimmer exercises, thus having to work much harder.

OPPOSITE, TOP LEFT Exercise pools are frequently used in conjunction with cycling or cross-training machines to give a full physical workout.

OPPOSITE, TOP RIGHT Some water aerobic exercises can be assisted by holding onto the side of a pool or steps, for example while doing a series of leg exercises or sideways kicks. Here, graduated steps and extended rails provide plenty of variety in water depth and levels.

OPPOSITE, BOTTOM LEFT Large areas of glass panels have been used to bring light into this narrow pool, but it is vital that the panels fit well to prevent cold air from coming in and hot damp air escaping to adjacent rooms.

OPPOSITE, CENTER Although long and narrow, this outdoor lap pool is ideal for swimming lengths and aerobic exercise.

OPPOSITE, BOTTOM RIGHT A jet pool set in a wooden deck can be heated and protected, with a cover for year-round use.

ABOVE LEFT A large expanse of glass makes a room feel fresh and creates a link with the outdoors, but condensation can be a problem, which may also have an adverse affect of exercise machines so this must be dealt with by using an efficient dehumidifying system.

ABOVE RIGHT Glass skylights have been used to allow daylight into this basement pool. The decorative focus is on exercise and easy maintenance rather than entertaining or leisure.

pool and gym complex

Built at one end of a series of colonnaded rooms in a restored building on the outskirts of Venice, Italy, this pool and Jacuzzi are a frequently used part of a family's health and fitness regime. The pool is an integral part of the main house and can be clearly seen from the entrance and the hallway.

The huge arched windows and pivoting doorways of the ground floor pool room are custom-made from extra-clear, glare-reduced SVP glass, and they allow the pool to be opened during fine weather but firmly sealed and heated in winter. The door to the hallway is edged with a rubber seal to give a snug fit so the moisture and heat don't escape into the rest of the house.

The dramatic curving yellow staircase, which seems more vivid against the blue of the pool, has treads of ebony made from recycled South African railroad ties. The walls are finished in Marmorino, a handmade typically Venetian plaster of polished marble dust. The marble is ground five times, and when the surface has dried, it is polished to a silky-smooth finish with soap.

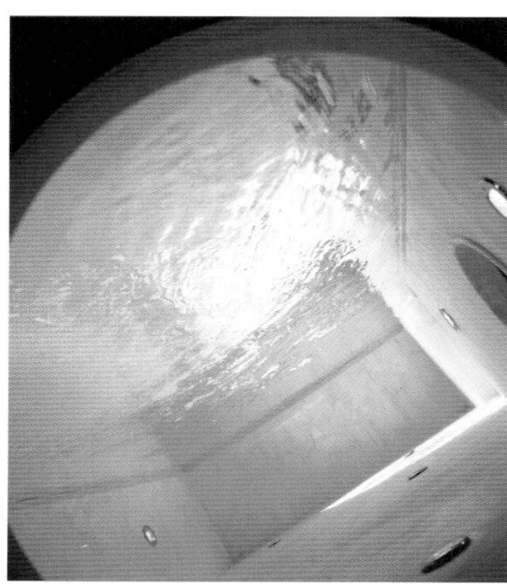

ABOVE Underwater jets can be switched on to give the pool water more vibrancy and motion, which makes it more interesting and challenging to swim in.

RIGHT The pool fits exactly into the main part of the restored colonnade, while the Jacuzzi and sitting area are arranged in an adjacent area covered with white stone.

OPPOSITE A submarine-type view of the pool is seen through the 2½in (6cm)-thick tempered and reinforced glass porthole panels in the basement spa, gym, and sauna room.

ABOVE The pool can be clearly seen from the main hallway of the house and is an integral part of the decorative plan. The bright blue of the water sets off the vivid yellow of the sensually curving staircase.

ABOVE RIGHT The ample use of glass throughout the pool complex, both as internal panels and on many of the exterior walls, makes the whole space feel light and fresh—a real incentive for exercise.

In the basement area, reached by a staircase at the side of the pool, there is an open-plan shower, gym, sauna, and changing room. This exercise area can be viewed through a series of reinforced glass portholes set into the pool wall below the water level. At night the lights, also recessed into the walls by the portholes, illuminate the pool like a giant light box, which can be viewed as a feature from the dry, subterranean room, giving the feeling and appearance that the room itself is submerged.

The extensive use of glass in the design of the pool and basement rooms gives the whole wing a feeling of light, and it is invigorating for those who use it. The large-scale external glass panels also look out over gardens and woodland, which gives a changing and seasonal view.

Pool size
13ft (4m) wide by 30ft (9m) long by 4ft (1.35m), sloping to 4½ft (1.45m) deep

Construction
A reinforced concrete base with the pool lining and surround finished in white Istrian stone

What material was used on the ceiling?
Girders of Canadian Hemblock wood

Filtration and cleaning
Quartz sand with isocyanate trichloride and calcium hypoclorite

Special feature
All the glass panels, doors, and windows are custom-made with reinforced glass and those on the outer walls of the house are treated with an antiglare finish

OPPOSITE The Jacuzzi's rounded front face has been used as part of the surround design and forms one side of the built-in steps. The rounded aspect breaks up the overall linear outline of the pool.

DESIGN AND DECOR

Design and decoration are about fun and indulgence. It's the reward after dealing with the practical aspects of pool location and maintenance. A pool is a place to enjoy yourself, and its design, although primarily safe and nonobstructive, should reflect that. The colors and embellishments of the pool and its surroundings could make references to a hobby or pastime such as rowing or sailing, follow an historic legend or subject such as a Bacchanalian grotto or Roman tepidarium, indulge in a luxurious and exotic theme such as a Balinese spa, or be a place to display a striking mural or impressive sculpture. The sculpture could be a specially commissioned piece that doubles as a water feature, one that incorporates part of the aeration and water recycling system, so that it is not only beautiful, but useful, too.

You could also follow ethical ideals and inclinations and create a chemical-free, low-energy, environmentally friendly pool that will encourage the proliferation of plants and pond life. It is possible to convert an existing outdoor pool to this type of filtration method, and it is often a good way of re-using a pool that has fallen into disrepair. The latest trends and newest styles in pool design may also inspire you—materials such as steel and glass are finding favor, and advances in reinforcements and the mechanics of pump and filtration systems mean that pools can be put into even more unusual and unlikely locations than ever possible before.

themed pools

Themed pools are generally easier to take to the limits of their potential in an indoor location where walls and ceilings are included in the decoration, but outdoor pools can be themed, too. Outdoor pools will rely heavily on planting and structural features such as walls or fencing to bring the look together. For example, a desert oasis theme can be capitalized on by planting succulents and palms (avoid cacti because of the prickles) and a wall finished in the adobe shade of sun-dried bricks. Terra-cotta water pots and urns could also be planted and the perimeter of the pool finished with rounded pebbles embedded in concrete. A ziggurat tile border around the edge of the pool will help to bring the pool into the wider picture. Indoors, a pool room can become virtually anything from a tented pavilion to an Aztec temple, but the decoration should be water- and condensation-proof. Avoid hanging great swathes of fabric that will absorb dampness, and do not place anything at the pool edge that might be an obstacle or hinder getting in or out of the water. Glass is best used in its laminated and reinforced form, and should be stationary rather than movable. If you are looking for transparency, try unbreakable alternatives to glass, such as rigid plastic.

Lighting is an important ingredient in creating the right mood, but the lighting should never be so dim that it is difficult to see or find the pool edge. Encased and sealed lights recessed into walls, both in and out of the water, can be used to create a whole range of effects, and tinted bulbs under the water will change the perceived color of the whole pool (see pages 156–8).

OPPOSITE Three rowing oars, hung like trophies on a plain wall, create a subtle but attractive water-linked theme to the room.

ABOVE LEFT A modern sculptural feature brings color and texture to the side of a plunge pool.

ABOVE CENTER This period pool in a round building is extensively decorated with pillared balustrades and arched columns on a grand scale.

ABOVE RIGHT Take inspiration from some of the earliest pools, constructed by the Romans. Here the pale stone reflects light from the overhead grille and classic Doric columns.

RIGHT The walls and ceiling of this tented room are painted. The width and color of the stripes were copied from the fabric that is used to cover the doorways, and along the inner wall there is a mural depicting a riverside scene, so it appears that you are in a tent overlooking a river.

PREVIOUS PAGE The rocky landscape has been used as a basis for the design of this pool and its perimeter. A curving wall wraps around the steps from the house and the pool edge is irregular and highlighted by large lumps of stone.

an eastern retreat

LEFT In one of the recessed niches in the basement, a spa tub area has been created. The edge of its water overlaps with that of the main pool.

OPPOSITE A second recess houses a stone shelf supporting three finely carved Buddha heads. These busts help to set the tone of tranquillity and relaxation that should be enjoyed in the spa pool.

This pool was tailor-made to fit within the limits of the basement footprint of an urban house. The Orientally inspired pool and spa has a tranquil atmosphere and was designed as an escape from the bustle of work and life on the upper floors.

The walls and sunken pool and tub areas have all been covered in the same dark Portuguese limestone, giving a unity to the space and making it seem larger and more spacious than it is in reality. The darkness of the area also helps to enhance the feeling of relaxation, calm, and womblike security.

Within a windowless basement, the arrangement of artificial light is of primary importance. A grid of recessed ceiling lights attracts the eye upward and makes the ceiling appear more distant, whereas the series of lights focused on the stone shelf supporting the three Buddha heads is there to emphasize their serenity and the aura of calm they inspire. Small touches such as the bowl of miniature white orchids and the bell-based candleholder help to carry the Eastern theme throughout the pool room.

Pool size
18ft (5.37m) wide by 41ft (12.5m) long by 4½ft (1.35m) deep

Construction
Reinforced concrete

What material was used on the ceiling?
Painted plaster

What tiles were used?
Portuguese limestone

How is condensation dealt with?
Fresh-air heating, ventilation, and dehumidification system

Any acoustic work done?
Acoustic attenuation is included in the air-handling system

Heating system
Water-to-water heat exchangers fed from the household gas-fired boiler system

Filtration and cleaning
The pool water is filtered by medium-rate sand filters and purified by electronically generated ozone with a chlorine residual

BELOW Ecofriendly pools are wholly compatible with rural landscapes; it can be difficult to see where the wild and man-made environments meet.

OPPOSITE, TOP Even in an urban setting within the confines of a backyard the eco pool can be combined with decking and a rock feature to create a naturalistic environment.

OPPOSITE, BOTTOM The separation between the filter zone and swimming area can be clearly seen in this pool, accessed by wooden platforms.

eco pools

Using biotechnology, natural pools replicate the ecosystem found in a pond and use plants and microorganisms to filter the water and prevent algae from growing. The advantages of these pools is that there is no smell or taste of chlorinated water, they require a minimal amount of energy to function, and the water is kinder to the skin, especially for people with allergies or irritations.

Creating an eco pool starts with excavating a hole with a flat base. The filter zone needs to be equal to the swimming area, so these pools are large, on average 500 sq ft (50 sq m). The hole is lined with a heavy rubber sheet laid over a cushioned underlay at an average depth of 6½ft (2m).

The liner remains uncovered in the swimming area, but in the filter zone it will be bedded down with a layer of a medium such as washed gravel, sand, and lime mix, in which the plants can embed. A barrier between the two zones should be installed at a height that rises to about 4in (10cm) below the water surface. This contains the plants and heavier debris that will naturally gather toward the base of the pool. A pump system draws the water from the filter zone, and skims and filters it before pumping it into the swimming area; and water from the swimming area is then pumped back into the filter zone for cleaning. It is essential that the water is constantly circulated between the two zones.

Pool size
Can vary, but a dip pool should be no less than 100 sq ft (10 sq m) and an average swimming pool is 500 sq ft (50 sq m)

Construction
A rubber "skin" with protective padding at the pool base

Filtration and cleaning
These pools are built with underwater walls for separating the swimming and cleaning areas. In the cleaning area the base is half filled with a special soil that encourages the growth of water plants. The used water runs through this plant or reed bed and then through a skimmer, where the water is cleaned of plant and insect debris before it is pumped back into the recreation pool. No chemicals are required

What power is used?
Only a minimal amount of electricity for the water pump—the sun heats the water

Special feature
Planted to blend in with the landscape, and beds mostly contain plants that fit the look of the vegetation in the pool

garden pond pool

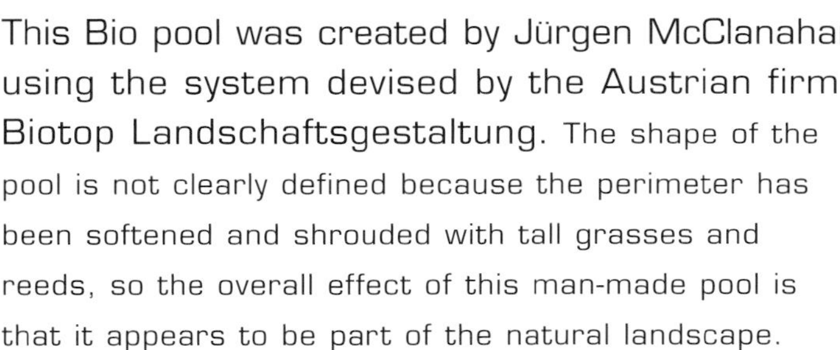

This Bio pool was created by Jürgen McClanahan using the system devised by the Austrian firm Biotop Landschaftsgestaltung. The shape of the pool is not clearly defined because the perimeter has been softened and shrouded with tall grasses and reeds, so the overall effect of this man-made pool is that it appears to be part of the natural landscape.

When planning this pool, McClanahan deliberately landscaped the surrounds to be compatible with its environs; but in other locations he has used pebbles, stones, sand, and rock to give the appearance of a creek, and in urban settings he has constructed patios made of flagstone and a number of wooden decks to suit the style of those locations.

OPPOSITE The inner wall that separates the filtration bed from the clear swimming water is visible when standing on the surrounding bank.

ABOVE The pool is large and encircles a tree that has been preserved on an island of land.

LEFT The island is connected to the "mainland" by a picturesque wooden bridge.

RIGHT An overly long lap pool is part of the architectural design of this modern, winglike structure. The water can be used for swimming; but when not being used, its long, narrow configuration accentuates the building's appearance.

future pools

Moving rapidly on from the ubiquitous turquoise-lined rectangle, modern pools are fast changing in color, shape, and construction. Color is one of the most notable areas, with the current divide between the natural look and the opulent. The natural appearance focuses on stone, pebbles, or beige, gray, or green liners and finishes, while the luxury look homes in on jetblack mosaics, shadow effects (where the base is a deep shade of a color such as cobalt blue but gradually lightens in tone as it reaches the surface), and metallic insets. Shapes have become less formal and rigid and now veer toward the organic or unusual, often customized to suit a site or landscape. Length or lap pools know no bounds; they are longer and more architectural, part of a structural feature rather than solely a swimming space.

Lighting is used to change the color of the pool between day and night or for special occasions. Tinted gels and filters can be set to give a rainbow assortment of hues to the water. Fiber-optic lights are increasingly being recessed into pool floors so that at night they shine like a constellation of tiny stars. Pool accessories have also come into the 21st century, with stainless steel fire pits and polished stone fireplaces. Old wooden fences are replaced by color-rendered walls or reinforced glass panels, and sweaty plastic seats are rejected in favor of designer-label lounges.

LEFT Indoor–outdoor spaces, where the boundaries are blurred, make the pool part of the interior design and the internal rooms appear to be part of a larger landscape.

OPPOSITE This is without doubt a pool with a view. Built out on a cantilevered balcony, it is surrounded by transparent glass panels. Swimmers feel as though they are floating above clouds.

polished steel

ABOVE This is the view of the pool and deck as seen from one of the upper terraces. The sloping base at the deep end of the pool is clearly visible.

BELOW The clean lines of the pool are complemented by the neat planting, but the mesh blocks of jagged stone create an interesting textural contrast.

This pool, designed by architect Gunther Weidner, is on one of a series of hillside terraces cut into a garden in Austria. The walls of the terraces are retained by huge steel mesh boxes filled with large stones, and their formidable gray and angular appearance and sheer bulk act as a foil to the immaculate smoothness and sheen of the futuristic pool they border.

The pool itself is made from polished steel, which is smooth and pleasant to touch as well as relatively easy to clean. The steel panels were each specially formed and joined so that there are no protruding welds, rivets, or raised seams. The steps were also custom-made of steel, with a nonslip finish and set at a low gradient slope for easy access.

The water in the pool is at a height that joins and continues the line of the surrounding wooden terrace, and a small water circulation channel between the two is covered with a steel grid. Recessed into the pool walls and floor are several enclosed lights, a series of powerful water jets that can be used for massage or to swim against for a more powerful workout, and a pair of underwater sound speakers.

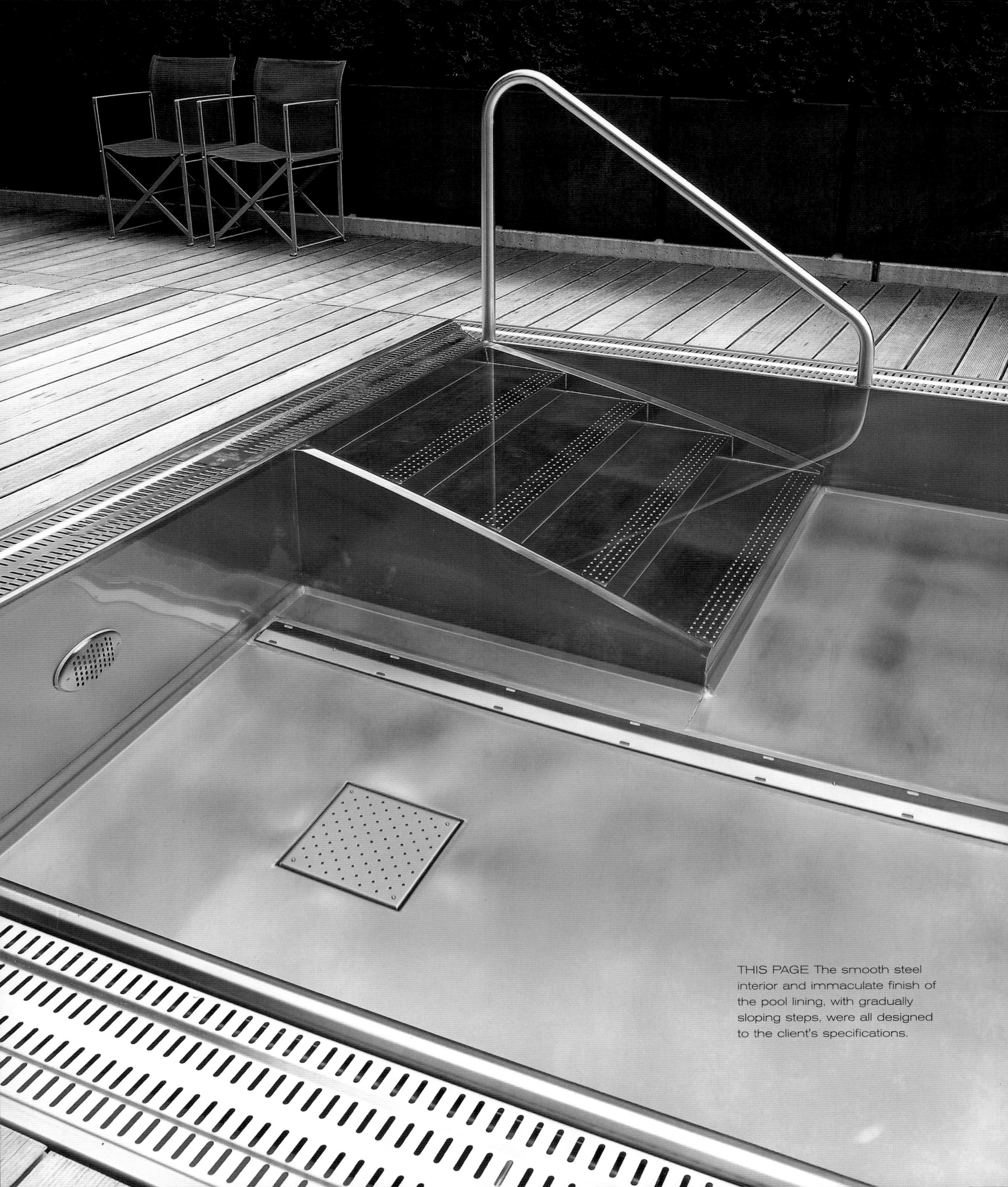

THIS PAGE The smooth steel interior and immaculate finish of the pool lining, with gradually sloping steps, were all designed to the client's specifications.

OPPOSITE, TOP LEFT One of the series of water jets installed in the pool walls; the water jets provide a strong jet of water ideal for massaging tired limbs.

OPPOSITE, CENTER Small enclosed lights cast beams across the water at night.

OPPOSITE, TOP RIGHT A basic outdoor shower area set into the wall is used for washing before and after swimming.

OPPOSITE, BOTTOM The pool was sited to make the most of the hillside views and to be protected from winds and weather. The boulder boxes on one side and the dense hedge provide protection and privacy.

BELOW The angular pool is a perfect counterbalance to the unusual round house it sits beside. The silvery steel finish also enhances the 1930s, nautical look of the house.

When the pool is not in use, a transparent roller cover seals it. The cover has a solar feature that allows heat from the sunshine to raise the water temperature and then retain it, but more conventionally, it also insulates and prevents heat loss overnight or at colder times of the year.

Arranged around the perimeter of the pool are an outdoor shower and a raised sunbathing deck overlooking the pool. The landscaping includes a long, thick wall of densely planted hedging, and the tops of the stone block retaining walls are filled with low, compact shrubs, specially chosen for their low leaf-shedding qualities.

Pool size
11½ft (3.5m) wide by 30ft (9m) long by 3ft 3in (1m) graduating to 4½ft (1.4m) deep

Construction
The pool is made from V2A polished steel sections, welded together to form a completely smooth surface, for aesthetic and safety reasons

Heating system
A mix of solar heat sourced from panels set into the roof of the house and electrical hot-water heating from the house's main central heating system

Filtration and cleaning
The sand filtration system is located in a separate underground pool house, along with the circulation pumps, and a mild chlorine solution is also used

Sound system
Sealed underwater speakers pump music directly into the water

Lighting
Underwater lamps are set into the sides of the pool

Special feature
Water jets can be used to swim against for a more vigorous aerobic workout, or for a massage

water features

Water features are increasingly a part of pool design. As a way of integrating a pool into the landscape, or in urban settings to make them more of a focal point and feature, displays of water are an exceedingly useful device. Pool water needs to be aerated and filtered as part of the circulation process, and it is a relatively simple matter to route the water through some sort of architectural feature, instead of allowing it to bubble directly back under the pool surface. You can direct it down a trough, allow it to tumble down a rock, propel it through a steel shoot, or let it cascade in a sheet down a wall like a waterfall.

In addition to making a practical contribution to pool maintenance, the redirected water will be a feature to please the senses: the sound of running water is a relaxing background noise; the ripples and waves it causes are entertaining to the eye; and if you are in the pool, the tumbling water can be used as a massage jet, as a refreshing shower, or as an endless source of splashing fun for playing children. Introducing movement to the water can bring an added dimension to any style of pool, but it is particularly useful for a uniformly shaped pool that might otherwise be a little dull.

Water features can also have an exciting nightlife. Lit by strategically placed and focused spotlights, the running water will be highlighted as a focal point, even in a small urban yard. The effect is to draw the eye out and to create interest beyond the immediate environment, making any space seem larger.

ABOVE LEFT The angled spout from which the filtered water returns to the pool slopes gently down, which softens the sound by reducing the height from which the water falls.

ABOVE RIGHT A trio of low, slotted vents produces a regularly spaced flow of water that add surface interest to this plain, symmetrical pool.

LEFT A low, flat rock creates a link between the pool and its rocky surroundings.

RIGHT Several small jets will make a lighter sound whereas a solid wall will be louder.

ABOVE Colored tiles and sculptural steel spheres are part of a whole design plan that works with the low wall containing a lateral cascade.

RIGHT A wall of craggy rock is broken up with a meandering painted panel at the top of which is a water spout. The painted section of wall blurs the outline of the pool edge, making it appear to be irregular and higher than it is.

BELOW A slim upright water feature, such as this tiled wall, is a perfect accessory to a narrow lap pool in an urban setting.

LEFT The encircling wall borders the pool with its water feature, the rough wood deck, and the ancient milkwood tree. The texture of the wall surface, deck, and water are part of the overall design that reflects the surrounding landscape.

OPPOSITE The projecting wall is punctured by a doorway through which the terrace continues around the pool. Eucalyptus fencing poles have been used to create rotating screens along the front of the house and poolside.

sculptural waterfall

This pool and sculptural curving wall were designed by architect Seth Stein. Within the wall's protective wrapping are the simple rectangular pool, the deck area, and the house, also created by Stein, and an ancient milkwood tree. The buildings and pool surround have deliberately been finished with materials that provide textural variation and pick up on the location of the pool, overlooking the dunes and beach on the southern cape of South Africa.

The end of the encircling wall terminates as it projects 6½ft (2m) into the water, and from a channel in its upper edge, water falls over a flat stone spout into the pool. The flat stone forces the water to fan out into an attractive arch, which also provides an excellent back and shoulder massage for anyone standing underneath it at the shallow end of the pool.

The varied and contrasting textures comprise of the surface of the water itself, the many surrounding concrete surfaces, the rough wooden decking, and the eucalyptus fencing sticks that are bound into pivoting blinds on the façade of the building.

Pool size
16ft (5m) wide by 40ft (12m) long by 3ft 3in graduating to 6ft (1 to 2m)

Construction and finish
Concrete retaining wall with natural concrete render in a local natural sandy color; the aquamarine is the reflected color of the sky

Heating system
Electrically operated heating and pump system

Filtration and cleaning
Pump and saline filters

Special feature
Local materials and colors were used to make the pool and surround harmonious with the setting

FINISHING

OUR POOL

The location and landscaping of pools is about the way they are used and their overall appearance, but in this section we go into the more specific details. We examine the actual ingredients that go intomaking the pool itself, such as the various types of structures, their sizes and shapes, colors, and finishes, as well as immediate surroundings—which include walkways, decks, and patios—and the accessories and furniture that are suitable to be used on them.

The safety, maintenance, and running of your pool, including its lighting and heating, are worth studying in some depth, because they will affect the quality of the water and therefore have a direct impact on your enjoyment of it. A pool that is neglected or badly maintained may become dogged with algae or mold problems; in the worst cases the water could become contaminated or toxic.

With a new pool you may need to let the water partially fill and drain so that any residue of builder's dust can be flushed away. A freshly filled pool may also need to be left for a day or two for the water to settle before you can check the water quality and work out your maintenance schedule. There are many home testing kits available to show the pH and alkaline levels, or the work can be done under contract by a commercial pool company. If you do it yourself, make sure you take the sample from around 18in (45cm) below the surface and avoid taking it from directly in front of the pumps or water return pipes, because this water will be freshly filtered and aerated and not wholly representative of the main body of water. Hot tubs, spas, and Jacuzzis should also be regularly maintained and the water quality tested to make sure it is clean, fresh, and pleasant to sit in.

LEFT The structure of this recessed basement pool will benefit from the support given by the earth that surrounds it, but the walls must be well waterproofed and insulated to prevent damp from seeping through the tiles and paint.

OPPOSITE, TOP LEFT This raised pool is built above ground so its walls don't have any earth support. With this sort of design, it is important to get an engineer involved as you will need to calculate the pressure exerted by the water to make sure the structure is strong enough to support and contain it. Here, the landscaping has been designed to directly link the pool into its surroundings, but with overhanging branches there will be some leaf fall.

OPPOSITE, TOP RIGHT This regular rectangular pool has been subdivided to provide a linear lap pool for exercising and a deep hot tub to unwind in. The water in the two areas may overlap, but the temperature of the lap pool should be cooler than that of the tub.

OPPOSITE, BOTTOM Built in an annex, this pool has ample space for family swimming. It has an adjacent spa and a wide perimeter area for recliners.

pool and tub types

When you decide to build a pool, you will have to select which type of construction best suits your needs. This choice will be influenced by location, suitability, and, if outdoors, climatic conditions. For example, in cool climates such as northern Europe and Scandinavia, it is advisable to insulate a pool within the shell construction to cut down on heat loss and to maintain the temperature, whereas in southern Mediterranean or tropical locations this additional layer is often unnecessary.

Other factors to take into consideration are the number of people who will use the pool, which may in turn help to determine its size. Also keep in mind the type of activity that will most frequently take place there. If the pool is primarily for cooling off and for children to play in, it doesn't need to be especially deep or big, whereas if it is intended for regular exercise, length is important because it is frustrating to have to turn after only half a dozen or so strokes, and the depth will need to be adequate for water aerobics or similar workout regimes.

The base of a pool can be level or graduated. If you choose a level pool bottom that is adequate for swimming but not for diving, you must make this clear with notices or warnings that the pool is shallow. Similarly, if your pool is deeper at one end than the other, sometimes referred to as a "dynamic" style—either because the floor of the pool is graduated or has two distinct depths—it should be clear to anyone who approaches which end is which.

You can build a pool above or below ground. Permanent raised pools are more usually constructed outdoors, often to take advantage of a view or setting, and they can be set into a deck or partially landscaped into a hillside on one or more sides so the bulk of the structure is not too dominant.

For pools that have been excavated and sunk into the ground, therefore having the added insulation and support of surrounding earth banks, there are a number of lining options. For example, you can have a frame made from a number of materials, such as steel, aluminum, sheets of rigid plastic, or treated and impregnated wood. The elements of the frame are nailed, screwed, and bonded together, then placed into the excavated recess. The sections are then joined and secured by transverse beams, which are firmly concreted into the ground.

The bottom of the excavated pool area is usually made from well compacted sand and overlaid with a layer of insulation before the pool membrane or vinyl liner is installed, and the supplier of the membrane will often recommend the type of frame most suitable to be used with the product. This type of frame and liner pool should be kept filled with water during the winter to prevent the membrane from shrinking or deteriorating. Liner pools are generally less expensive to construct than a tiled concrete pool.

Block constructions, using preformed concrete or insulation blocks, are an increasingly popular form of pool building. Blocks are built up in rows in the same way as a standard brick wall, and the surface is then skimmed with smooth plaster so nothing will puncture a plastic membrane. If the interior is to be tiled or lined with a stronger facing, the plaster finish can be rougher. This type of construction can be used both indoors and out, as well as set above or below ground.

Reinforced concrete offers the most flexible option for pool design because it can be poured between shutters or wooden boards that mark out any shape, so curves and irregular designs are easy to create. Concrete is also durable and will withstand a

wide range of temperature variations, but an important factor to bear in mind is that all pipes, ducts, and filters should be placed into the concrete before it sets, during construction.

Fiberglass pools are delivered to you as a complete form ready to be inserted and bedded down in a prepared site. Fiberglass is comparatively lightweight, but it has a certain brittleness so that when it is set into the ground, the sand bed, usually around 2in (5cm) deep at the base, must be level. Otherwise, when the water is poured into the pool, the weight may be unevenly distributed, causing the fiberglass shell to crack.

As the weight of the water increases in the pool, the sand will compress, so additional backfilling may be required, and because fiberglass pools are delivered to your home in a single preformed shape, don't forget to check that there is adequate access for a truck or crane to be able to deliver the pool to the site.

Hot tubs can be a separate entity or an integral part of a pool; they can also be sunk into the ground or set above it. A pool-and-tub combination will be installed at the same time and can be formed in concrete with a tiled finish or preformed in a single continuous fiberglass shape, so that the materials are one and the same. The machinery, pumps, piping, and ducting can also be plumbed in simultaneously, although the heat, pump, and sanitation requirements of the tub will be different from those of the main pool and will require separate controls.

Above-ground tubs or spas are usually constructed from a preformed acrylic, fiberglass, or thermoplastic shell. Between the liner and the exterior wall, there will be layers of insulation, piping, and electrical wiring. The above-ground spa must be set on a firm base and preferably on a ground-floor or reinforced upper level. Although the dimension of the tub may not be large and the structure comparatively light, when filled with water the total weight will be significant. For example, a 7-by-9ft (2.2-by-2.7m) spa can weigh in excess of 5,000 lbs (2. 5tons) when full.

UPDATING AND MODIFYING

If you have an existing pool or have inherited one with your home, it is possible to update and modify the facility as well as its surroundings. Once the pool is drained, you can have the interior examined to establish the structure and composition; a pool designer, architect, or installation company can then advise you on what remedial or decorative solutions are possible.

If your pool has a vinyl or similar lining, it is a relatively inexpensive and quick process to change it, but if the pool has a mosaic or tiled surface, the task will be more involved and time consuming. Concrete or screed surfaces can be painted with a vinyl-based or water-compatible paint or in some cases covered with bonding or adhesive and then tiled over.

Existing outdoor pools can be converted to an ecofriendly swimming pond. But again this will depend on the base structure. Before embarking on any alterations, it is best to consult the manufacturer, supplier, or architect who built or supplied the structure. If they are not available, find a reliable contractor through an allied trade association. Don't try exploratory drilling or hammering into the pool wall yourself–you may hit pipes or electrical wiring, and cause irreparable damage to the pool wall or cause flooding by fracturing a pipe or valve.

OPPOSITE This octagonal hot tub has a preformed acrylic base that has been recessed into a slatted wooden deck that has been raised up to take advantage of the view over the treetops. The tub structure itself is light, but the volume of water will considerably increase its overall weight; therefore, the wooden structure will have to be reinforced with bracing to make it safe and secure. A hot tub is an ideal place to sit and admire a view; in a pool the emphasis tends to be on swimming lengths and moving around, so there may not be as much opportunity to simply sit and watch the world go by.

RIGHT This pool has been constructed from a preformed fiberglass shell set in under the rim of a wooden deck. The rectangular shape will have been bedded down in a layer of sand and leveled out to make sure the weight of the water is evenly distributed across the whole shell. The gentle curve at the top of the shell has been tucked under the edge of the decking for protection and to give a neater finish to the overall appearance of the pool. These preformed acrylic and fiberglass shells now come in a variety of colors and finishes, including a mosaic print and a graduated color shadow.

pool shapes

There are two basic types of pool shape—the regular and free-form designs. Regular shapes are generally geometric in outline, such as oblong, L-shaped, rectangular, and square, and they are mainly constructed using concrete or blocks. The blocks themselves being angular, they are more suited to straight-sided designs.

Free-form shapes can be like a figure-eight, teardrop, kidney, or square on one side while rounded on the other; they can be more interesting and organic and allow for a certain degree of flexibility when you are trying to fit a pool into an awkward shape. Free-form

ABOVE LEFT This unusual triangular-shaped pool makes the most of the available space and is an eye-catching feature in its surroundings.

ABOVE RIGHT Following the curves of the breaking waves and undulating coastline, this pool's shape has been devised to harmonize with its setting.

BELOW Organic shapes are softer and less predictable; almost any shape can be made using poured concrete.

OPPOSITE The sculptural and irregular shape of this pool has been created to follow the outline of the podlike structures that look out over the coastline as well as the pool.

shapes are also useful for family pools where a smaller, shallow play or "beach" area for children can be created at one end while a deeper area for adults to swim comfortably can be supplied at the other. Some free-form pool shapes can be bought in precast fiberglass; more complicated or custom-made shapes need to be constructed on-site using forms and poured concrete.

Above-ground and individual in-ground tubs are generally regular shapes, either round, square, or rectangular. As an integral part of a main pool, hot and spa tubs may be more free-form or teardrop shaped, but in general the shape is regular, because the water jets need to be evenly spaced to be effective.

OPPOSITE, TOP LEFT Though basically a rectangular pool, the rounded side wall softens the other angles and makes an easy progression and link to the round hot tub that is part of the outdoor pool panorama.

OPPOSITE, TOP RIGHT Following the outer perimeter of the building, this semicircular pool's soft, flowing lines endorse those of the structure it mimics.

OPPOSITE, BOTTOM LEFT Set into a stepped terrace, the outer edge of this pool follows the curve of the step while the inner section is straight.

OPPOSITE, BOTTOM RIGHT The round deck is sympathetic to the line of the curved pool that laps around it; soft, sensual shapes sit more comfortably in a natural landscape.

ABOVE Two shapes are again combined into one; the long, linear lap pool is teamed with a sweeping set of steps that have rounded walls, creating an off-beat and unusual outline.

RIGHT A raised pool with an infinity edge is tailor-made to suit its setting; it is constructed to fit in around the irregular face of an adjacent rock.

colors for pool interiors

ABOVE Dark colors help a pool to blend in with its environment rather than stand out. The sky color and the volume of water will also have an effect on the color the water appears to be.

BELOW Natural materials, such as slate and stone, are now increasingly popular as pool linings; they have an affinity with woodland, shoreline, and other organic surroundings.

The color of the interior of your pool or tub is important because it will affect the overall appearance of the structure and its setting. Although there is a certain Hollywood glamour associated with vivid turquoise pools, this color is not necessarily the best for all locations, and it can look garish in a small pool in plain, urban surroundings. Take a look at various colors before making your decision and also consider the material you will use. For example, a gray-green quartz aggregate may sparkle in sunlight but could look flatter and duller underwater than a similarly colored ceramic tile that has a reflective, glazed surface. If your pool is outdoors and set in a lush green landscape, greener tones or softer shades of beige and gray may be more in keeping.

With the appropriate finishes to make them water compatible, natural materials such as stone and slate can be used to line pools, and even black tiles, whether mat or shiny, offer an interesting alternative to the predictable shades of blue. Blue is the standard color for a pool interior because it is the color most commonly associated with water. But water always reflects the color of the sky, which on a sunny day will give it a degree of blueness anyway, so it can be more effective to select a color that enhances the pool in its surroundings rather than choose a color that clashes or stands out against it.

RIGHT Blue has been popular for pool linings for years, but now the trend is for the deeper hues, for cobalt and sapphire rather than vivid turquoise; and solid blocks of color are giving way to random mosaics or shadow effects. It is important to take the surroundings into consideration when selecting a color for the pool, not just the plants and trees, but also the structural elements such as decking and awnings; there should be a link or harmony in all aspects.

BELOW With an indoor pool you can be more adventurous with color, not just in the pool lining, but in the surroundings, too. A single pillar or wall of vivid color will make a statement and give the environment an upbeat and distinctive look. Lighting will also influence the way you see the color, for example, bright pink may look cooler and more vivid in natural light but warmer and redder under electric illumination.

For indoor pools, especially basements where there is little or no natural light, shades of blue are good because they create an illusion of light, sky, and the outdoors, and there are a variety of shades of blue that can be interesting and less predictable than turquoise. For example, rich, dark cobalt has depth and a jewel-like quality; or blue with a warming hint of pink, making a lavender hue, can be muted and relaxing, just as a refreshing powder blue can be invigorating. In these indoor locations you should select a color to endorse the feeling of the surrounding room and its décor. For example, if it is a space for a hot tub or wind-down zone, warm, soft hues would be appropriate; if the space is designed for exercise and for being energetic, a fresher mix of pale green and powder blue could be beneficial.

Colors such as red, yellow, and orange are rarely used as main colors in pool interiors. They can be included in a decorative mosaic or border trim; but because hot colors are associated with fire and heat, they are not really appropriate as a single color for a pool interior, as they jar in that particular setting.

However, contemporary optical and lighting effects mean that you can introduce temporary flashes of color to your pool's water—gels and filters can be applied to lights so that the water appears to be vivid pink or acid yellow, for example, which can be a fun way of "decorating" a space for a party or an evening event. With moving lights, different colors can be mixed and blended so that they appear to move over or under the water surface, while spots of beams highlight cartain areas. Larger washes of colored light can be used to accentuate or even to modify or drastically alter the pool's normal lining color for a short-lived change.

using pattern

You don't have to restrict yourelf to a single color in your pool—you can blend colors and make your own individual look by using mosaic tiles. For example, you can still have turquoise as a base, but make it appear more green by mixing it with tiles in mint, emerald, and racing green; or appear a richer blue by adding sapphire and even gray. To lift the color to a more zesty, modern, and fresh spectrum, try adding white and lime tiles.

The depth of the pool can also be indicated by graduating the color of the tiles so that the shade is lighter at the shallow end and darker where the water is deeper—this can also be a helpful safety device. Shadow effects can also be pleasing; these are achieved by using paler-colored tiles around the rim of the water surface, then gradually increasing the depth and intensity of color through to the bottom of the pool, where the darkest shade of all in your chosen spectrum is used.

Pattern can be introduced to otherwise single-color designs by incorporating a border or band. These trimmings, usually around the water's edge and on steps or ledges, can be a traditional Greek key or stylized wave, or something more original and ornate, incorporating a range of colors. Pictorial mosaics are sometimes used on a pool floor, and they can be a family crest or monogram or be inspired by an amphibious creature such as a turtle or dolphin. Inspiration can also be found in the décor of baths from Roman times, when mosaics were immensely popular.

Athough a single color throughout a pool can be effective, the mixing of colors may give a more natural and interesting appearance. Vinyl liners, the thick rubber sheets used with frames, used to be predominantly a flat, all-over turquoise shades, but now liners are available in a range of watery colors and printed with mosaiclike patterns and borders and faux tile bands.

TOP LEFT A grid of medium-sized mosaics in a single color will create a background that gives a feeling of depth as well as acting as a reflective mirror when the pool surface is still.

TOP RIGHT Pictorial mosaics have been popular since Roman times. Dolphins, with links to the sea and numerous myths, are frequently portrayed.

LEFT A more contemporary and abstract pattern shows wavelike patterns created from four colors of mosaic tiles.

OPPOSITE Natural stone such as slate has its own integral pattern, and when cut and laid in random directions, the slate appears to vary in hue and tone.

BELOW LEFT Ceramic tiles offer a wide scope of surface decoration. Here a mix laid in different directions makes a feature of an access area while also drawing attention to it as a safety measure.

BELOW RIGHT. A combination of large and small mosaic tiles decorate this pool. Large tiles give quicker, more economic cover, while mosaics are better on round shapes. Here, they highlight a raised hot tub.

OPPOSITE When choosing a material for an outdoor pool that will be subjected to extremes of temperature in summer and winter, check with the supplier that it is suitable for such a site.

materials

There is a wide range of materials to choose from when it comes to the décor of your pool, but they should be chosen in conjunction with the basic structure. For example, a wooden frame is designed to be used with a pool liner, and ceramic tiles, which are heavy, are best used with concrete or block-built structures.

Ceramic tiles come in a variety of sizes and finishes, such as glazed and matt. You can buy standard tiles suitable for pools from most retailers, or you could have them specially designed and produced. Small mosaic tiles are generally supplied on a mesh backing that makes them easier to install, especially over a large surface area. There are also glass mosaic tiles that have a clear top with a tinted background, and they cover a wide range of colors, including metallics such as gold and silver. Glass mosaics can be very effective around rims and edges, but the overall effect tends to be lost under very deep water.

Natural materials such as marble and stone can be used as a hard-wearing and weather-resistant finish; even rounded, smooth pebbles set into a concrete base will give a natural and environmentally pleasing appearance. Other materials, such as steel, can be preformed like a fiberglass shell and installed over an insulated base, but materials such as this will need a special bonding or lacquer for protection before filling with water.

There are also a number of paint finishes that can be applied directly over the smooth surface of a plastered or rendered wall. These paints must be specially developed to withstand the constant contact with water and applied by a specialist. Glassflake is one such product, and is so called because it is reinforced with glass flakes to increase its impermeability. There are around 125 layers of glass flake in every 1⁄16in (1mm) of pool paint lining, which is built up gradually in three layers.

LEFT AND OPPOSITE, TOP Durability is important for wood decking, so choose a timber that is strong and rot-resistant, such as cedar or redwood. Wood can be treated to make it more weatherproof and an impregnated moss inhibitor is also useful, as damp wood in shady areas can easily become slimy and slippery.

OPPOSITE, BOTTOM LEFT A surround of irregular flagstones links this pool to its garden environment and provides clean and easy access to the water, although stone can become hot underfoot when exposed to direct sunshine. Another problem with flagstones is that the area between them needs to be weeded, and this is best done by hand as sprays and solutions might seep into and affect the pool water.

OPPOSITE, BOTTOM RIGHT Try to configure the pool so that part of the deck or surround is under shade during the hottest part of the day. Mature trees and dense bushes are ideal, although they should be far enough from the pool to avoid leaf fall affecting the water. Make sure the deck is wide enough to accommodate chairs and lounges and for people to walk around easily.

decks, patios, and walkways

These recreational areas abut the pool and become part of its frame or infrastructure; they also contribute to the enjoyment of outdoor life. When planning the location of the pool or hot tub, these ancillary areas should also be taken into consideration. For example, with an outdoor pool or tub you may want to have a deck or patio area in the shade, or partial shade, and so set a little way back from the immediate pool surround. To reach the house or patio with ease, you may need a walkway—a smoothly surfaced path that can be walked on comfortably with bare feet, making it easy to move from one part of the pool area to another. An outdoor barbecue may also be sited around the pool area, but for safety reasons it should be at a distance from the water's edge.

Wood is a good material for walkways and decking, although it can be slippery when wet, so a ribbed or textured surface will be advantageous and also helps water drain away. Wood needs to be pretreated and regularly maintained to prevent it from warping, cracking, splintering, or becoming slippery with moss.

Wood is attractive in its natural state, but it can be painted or stained in a wide range of colors. Some of the stains have an integral preservative, which will help with overall durability. Wood stains can enrich and enhance the wood's own color, darken the wood or make it a different color such as green, red, or blue; but these stains will weather and bleach in sunlight, so in time will become paler than the original application.

Natural material such as granite, limestone, and sandstone, used in paving tiles and flagstones, are ideal for outside pool areas because they have an affinity with the location and are hard wearing and weather resilient. The maintenance problem that occurs with paving slabs is primarily the area between them, where sand, gravel, or concrete grout is laid. These joint areas are where weeds and wild grasses take hold; and being close to a pool it is unwise to spray them with chemicals, so it is either down on your hands and knees with a fork or an eco-friendly alternative to the spray, such as salt. The way to avoid, or at least cut down on, the weed problem is to lay a polyurethane membrane under the bed of sand before the flagstones are laid.

Concrete is versatile and economic, and can be finished with either a rough or smooth surface, or topped with embedded pebbles or rounded pea gravel. Bricks are also good in outdoor locations, and their warm red coloring, like terra-cotta tiles, can be a good link to a building or wall in a similar material. Bricks can also be laid in a variety of patterns such as herringbone, diagonal herringbone, lines, and boxes.

If you want to create a link between an indoor room and the outdoors, your choice of material may be predicated by what is suitable for both. Wood can be laid as polished boards or parquet inside and treated decking beyond the French or sliding doors. Sometimes a different finish will be the answer; for example, the dark sandstone Pietra Serena can be used indoors, but it will require a flamed finish and protective seal for external use.

With indoor pools, specifying the flooring means taking three factors into consideration first—safety, aesthetics, and utility. Maintenance and cleaning are especially important in an enclosed space, and because there is a limited amount of cooling and drying fresh air, the slip safety factor is even more important than in an outdoor location. Some surfaces such as stone can accrue a

build-up of algae or organic material on the surface. A microscopic layer of residue human body fat and dead skin detritus can decrease the friction coefficient of a material and therefore affect its safety. Consult your stone supplier about the best effective cleaning and maintenance regime for that particular surface.

Smooth surfaces should be sealed or glazed to make them water-resistant as well as impervious to staining from substances such as oil, sun preparations, and drink spills.

You can also make a smooth surface safer to walk on with wet feet by laying a path of ribbed or mesh rubber matting. From a safety point of view, abrasive surfaces are good and have a low slip factor, but the downside is that they are less comfortable to bare feet and difficult to clean thoroughly.

There are a number of remedial products that can be used if you have an existing slippery floor surface or have put one down that is proving to be so. Low viscosity antislip coating increases the good grip factor on marble and terrazzo flooring without affecting the stones' appearance, but these preparations are not suitable for use on nonporous surfaces.

A traditional floor covering and pool surround is marble—it has been used widely from Roman times and in Turkish baths and hammams. Marble floors are good to use in conjunction with underfloor heating, which warms the stone and helps moisture to evaporate, making it warm and safe to walk on. Granite and a number of other hard stones can also be used this way.

ABOVE RIGHT A narrow border of rounded pebbles is a soak-away and a visually interesting break between the pool and its surroundings. The pebbles are ideal because they are smooth underfoot; aggregate stone and crushed shells look attractive, but they have sharp edges.

RIGHT A pool surround can be made of several finishes; here, a checkerboard of tiles is combined with an area of mixed mosaics edged with a regular border of single-colored mosaic. By mixing the size of tile and the arrangement of colors, you can create an interesting border and "beach."

OPPOSITE, TOP LEFT With an organic or free-form pool, the edge should follow the pool's outline. Here, smoothly surfaced stone paving slabs have been cut and finished to complement the pool's shape. A plain stone is better for a pool with a complex shape because a highly decorative surround will distract from the pool's outline.

OPPOSITE, TOP RIGHT Groups of four terra-cotta paving slabs are outlined with infill of rounded pebbles embedded in concrete. The contrast of stone and tile is unusual, as is the textural mix of the round and the flat surfaces.

OPPOSITE, BOTTOM LEFT A broad band of narrow, smooth slabs, sloping slightly toward the water, provides not only a pathway around the rim, but also access and a sitting area.

OPPOSITE, BOTTOM RIGHT Brick is versatile—it may be laid in a variety of ways to create shapes and pattern. It makes a good pool surround in front of a period brick-built house because façade and surround will be similar in color.

ABOVE In an indoor pool such as this, the surround can be underheated. Heated flooring can be an integral part of the overall system and will do away with the need for radiators.

LEFT As part of the garden landscape, this pathway has been chosen to blend in with the surroundings while providing an easy surface to walk on.

OPPOSITE, TOP LEFT This path of black volcanic stone is a feature of the pool, leading directly over it and in contrast to the pool's pale, smooth finish.

OPPOSITE, TOP RIGHT A stepping-stone arrangement of wooden blocks projects out from the pool's wooden deck, creating a viewing point for a bather or fully clothed person.

OPPOSITE, BOTTOM On a large pool an elevated walkway cuts down the legwork of getting from one side to another. It doubles as a sunbathing platform.

LEFT The pump room for this pool is discreetly concealed in an adjacent all-purpose room, where all the machines such as the heater, filter, and pumps as well as the chemicals and replacement filters can be easily accessed but not seen.

RIGHT Skimmer baskets and poolside filters must be regularly cleaned. These are recessed into the pool surround, but camouflaged and protected under lids cut from the same stone.

RIGHT OPPOSITE Drainage grates should be located right beside the pool rim so that any overflow water can pass through them and be recycled; they also help to prevent insects and animals from reaching the water.

cleaning and drainage

Filtration systems are available that employ a number of different catalysts, such as sand, salt, and diatomaceous matter (fossilized plankton skeletons), which strain and clean the water as it passes through. Salt or saline filtration is increasingly popular because it utilizes a natural substance with iodine and antiseptic qualities; it is also a useful option for those who wish to choose a more environmentally friendly system than traditional chemicals.

Ozone generators purify the water and kill bacteria using a minimal amount of chlorine. With a privately owned pool that is regularly used by a number of different people, some chlorine many be necessary, though the amount required will be significantly less than for a conventionally filtered pool, so there should be no red eyes or bleach-scented swimwear.

The maintenance of the filter is of prime importance because it will regulate the quality of water you are swimming in. Each manufacturer will prescribe specific procedures for that particular filter and will make specific recommendations as to the frequency of cleaning required, and most filter systems have a built-in warning or alert system that will indicate when additional or emergency cleaning is necessary. Regular maintenance of the pool machinery and water is important, because if there is a problem, it can escalate over time and build up to be something that requires a more radical remedy. By setting aside little more than half an hour a week, it should be possible to test and clean the water of an average outdoor family pool. If even this sounds daunting, you can also take out a maintenance contract with a pool company, which will then come and check the levels of chemicals and undertake the necessary care program for you.

Drainage around a pool or hot tub is necessary to prevent flooding and to recycle the excess water. Overflow gratings are used to protect the drain or gulley while allowing the water ample and easy access so that it can be cleaned and pumped back into the pool. Generally the drainage and gratings run around the perimeter of the pool and act as an interface between the surround and the pool edge. Gratings come in a number of materials, such as stainless steel and high-quality PVC. They are available in a variety of widths to suit various areas, also in straight and curved sections and in colors to blend with the pool and its surround. Grates should be easily removable so the drainage system below can be regularly cleared and cleaned; human matter such as hair can often tangle up the filters, and outside there will be leaf and plant debris as well as insects and litter. For this reason they usually come in sections so they can be lifted easily. The grates may also be used to cover and protect pipework and machinery such as filters, allowing air to circulate around the machinery and keep it cool. Grates can also be used to create barrier-free areas around a shower, indoor or outdoor, so that you can walk straight under a showerhead and the excess water will be ducted away rather than collected in a tray or trough.

Although some types of pools need to be drained during the winter, it is not always necessary. Nowadays many pools are equipped with a frost-stat control sensitive to a fall in temperature. When the temperature falls below a certain level, the frost-stat activates the filter pump, which circulates the water, bringing the warmer water from the bottom to the top. The circulation of the water, and its movement, prevents the buildup of ice.

highlights and features

Features linked to a pool, such as ancillary water displays and lighting, can produce spectacular results. This is very much a part of the general contemporary trend to make pools integral with their environment, but also to give them a 24-hour life, with an after-hours' role as a decorative, evening attraction. Water features such as spouts, waterfalls, and cascades can help to link the pool to the surrounding landscape, as well as adding another dimension to the predominately single-level surface area. Water features can be raised above the pool surface, mounted on a wall, or located on top of a column so that there is the added aural dimension of the sound of falling water, as well as the visual wave effect caused by the water hitting the surface below. These features can be a simple ledge, an arrangement of rocks, or a more sculptural object, such as a stainless steel spout or a special commission from an artist. They may also be highlighted by spot or feature lighting so that they are illuminated at nightfall.

The use of infinity pool edges, which have no clearly defined physical rim so that the water appears to "disappear" or merge into its surroundings, is another way of incorporating a pool into its environment. Infinity edging also makes the pool appear larger because it does not seem to be restricted or defined by a definitive border, but blends smoothly with the skyline.

With narrow pools beside a wall or those located directly outside the French windows or sliding doors of a house, a wall-mounted waterfall or aqua sculpture will create a pleasant aspect on which to look out. The tumbling water can be filtered and recycled so that it is part of the pool's main water feed and linked to its pump and filter mechanisms. At night, innovative modern lighting such as fiber-optics can be used to create an array of patterns and designs, with changing colors playing over the moving water. Or certain areas of the wall and water can be enhanced with a variety of single-color spotlights.

LEFT The sound and movement of water is an attractive addition to a pool. Here, a small trough pours cleaned water back into the pool and is an integral part of the water purification cycle. Keep the size of your water feature in proportion to the scale of the pool and gauge the height, force, and fall of the water so that it is pleasant to listen to rather than a headache-inducing downpour.

OPPOSITE This three-level cascade pours water into a series of round bowls that emphasize the shape of the surrounding round windows; the water then enters the pool. This small feature would not be able to recycle all the water for a pool this size, so another main filter and recycling pump is located elsewhere. To create the sound of rapidly tumbling water, direct the flow through a high, steep, and narrow gap, whereas for a softer, more relaxing background sound, create a wide, slim curtain of water directed over low-level, smooth flat stones or ledges.

lighting and heating

OPPOSITE, TOP LEFT Lighting is directed to highlight the trees, which in turn are reflected in the pool's surface for a magical view. All outdoor and pool lighting should be specifically for the purpose and wired for that use.

OPPOSITE, TOP RIGHT The lighting within the house shines out through two walls of glass screens and panels, and adds to the effect of the submerged lighting within the pool. The pool is clearly visible from the house as part of the larger design.

OPPOSITE, BOTTTOM LEFT Lighting in the raised plant bed, the house, and the pool bring all three elements together and make the pool and landscape seem larger and more dramatic than they appear in daytime.

BELOW This wall is a feature panel with strategically arranged lighting. Seen from the house, the panel is reflected in water, making it seem twice its size.

BELOW RIGHT An outdoor awning is edged with cascades of tiny lights. Fiber-optic lighting is increasingly popular for this type of lighting feature.

BOTTOM RIGHT Downlighters from the top of the wall draw the eye to the water, and the row of small lights creates a dappled effect on the surface.

There are two main areas for lighting: in the pool or spa tub and around it. In the case of an outdoor pool or tub, the perimeter lighting can be extended to include illumination that highlights features and planting in the landscape. At night, a light shining up into the branches of a graceful tree will make it a feature, and shadows against a wall or over the ground can give a feeling of depth and perspective to even a small patio garden or yard. Steps and pathways can also benefit from discreet, low-level lighting, which will make them easier and safer to walk on.

There are many types of outdoor electrical lighting, but the first step is to make sure that the technical side is correct. Lightbulbs should be encased or sealed in waterproof casings to protect them against moisture such as condensation or splashes from the pool and rain; all cables and wiring used should be safety approved and designed specifically for outdoor use, as should any switches or sockets that are located outside.

The 120-volt system widely used for outdoor lighting should be professionally installed, with cables buried in waterproof pipes or set above the soil or paving in insulated casing. Alternatively,

low-voltage outdoor lighting of 25 and 50 watts can be run via a transformer; this low-energy lighting can be very effective as secondary or mood lighting, but in itself it will not be strong enough to adequately light a whole pool area.

Among the various types of garden lights are those on plastic spikes that can be "planted" in the ground with the cable running to an outdoor power source; these can be moved around the yard to shine on specific areas when a particular plant or shrub is in bloom. Tall pillar lights are useful on steps and raised lawn edges, and can be permanently linked directly to an outdoor cable and run off a system from the main house or pool house.

There are light box cubes and traditional lanterns, such as cut-metal Moroccan lamps, that can be adapted to take an electrical fixture and will create intricate shadow patterns. Lights can also be concealed within terra-cotta pots or plant containers so they are not directly visible, but their illumination can be seen.

Candles are an attractive source of outdoor lighting, but they should be placed in tall-sided containers or lamp casings when positioned close to the pool itself, to prevent any injury or burns. Citronella and insect-repellent candles not only illuminate, but also help to keep bugs at bay; and tall flares, candles, or torches are a good way of bringing light in at different levels.

With indoor pools and hot tubs, you will have to adhere to the same safety standards; even though rainwater will not be a hazard, condensation will. In a basement pool where natural light is limited or nonexistent, electrical lighting will be essential and its location an important feature in creating ambiance and mood.

You may consider wall-mounted lights on a dimmer switch, or a system of two or three circuits of lights, so that when all are on there is maximum light but when just one circuit is in use, the level of light is low and intimate. These variable lighting systems allow you to change the mood from bright for sporting activity, such as an after-work swim, to low for evening relaxation and entertaining; but for safety reasons the lighting should never be so low or dim that you cannot clearly see the pool edge and the exit.

The other physical opportunity for lighting is within the pool or tub; this has two purposes, first, to make it safe to swim or take a spa dip at dusk or at night, and second, to highlight the pool or tub as a feature in its own right after dark.

The majority of spa tubs come with lighting as an integral feature, but for a swimming pool the most common form of lighting is enclosed in watertight casings, which are set into a recess or recessed directly into the pool walls and floor. To change the bulb, the casing is gently removed from the recess, or unscrewed from within the container and its rubber seal.

Increasingly popular is fiber-optic light, in which light is generated at one end of the cable and then "moves" along the reflective sides of the interior, so that the electrical source of light can be placed well away from the water and only the fiber-optic cable is in the water. The fiber-optic filaments can be used lengthwise to give a line of light or end-on to create small dots of light that look like a constellation of stars on the floor of a pool.

Most pools are heated using an integral heat exchange or boiler system, but costs can be cut significantly with the use of solar covers that pull over the pool surface when it is not in use and function as a large solar panel. Not only will the panel heat the water, but it will also keep the heat in because it seals the surface of the water off from the external air temperature. Solar covers are most useful for outdoor pools used mainly in summer, but can be used in conjunction with a boiler for year-round pool use.

It is also worth noting that it is best to keep the temperature of the pool water at just below body temperature so that it is invigorating and refreshing to swim in. Water that is overheated will make it feel as though you are relaxing in a bath, making you feel lethargic. If you are actively swimming and generating body heat, you will become increasing hot. The ambient temperature around an indoor pool should also be comfortable, both in a dry or wet swimsuit. An overheated room or environment will be stuffy and may in the long term aid the growth of fungi and bacteria, which thrive in warm, damp conditions.

OPPOSITE, LEFT Lateral lights directed from just under the pool surface illuminate the water rather than the area above it. This arrangement of lighting highlights the water itself and concentrates the eye on it without creating much vertical light pollution, which could be seen for miles around.

OPPOSITE, RIGHT Lighting below the water surface makes the pool appear to glow and gives it a softness that is in contrast with the hard stone surround and building.

RIGHT At nighttime the internal lighting in a pool allows any swimmers to gauge how deep the water is and to clearly see the pool edge and access; it is an essential safety feature as well as a decorative one.

BELOW A combination of rotating color downlighters and internal pool lights give this family basement pool space a very different atmosphere at night, making it far more of an adult zone, in contrast to its daytime appearance (see pages 98–101).

changing areas and showers

The changing area designated for a pool or tub will depend on its size, location, and use. For a small family pool or hot tub that is located close to the house, a separate changing facility may not be necessary. But for a larger pool, or a spa pool and tub arrangement in which you may progress from a swim to a steam room and on to a yoga mat or bicycle machine, a separate shower and changing facility can be beneficial.

For outdoor pools and tubs there are two options: either a permanent fixture or a temporary, seasonal arrangement. For a pool that is set at some distance from the house, perhaps linked to a barbecue or a patio entertaining space, a wood, stone, or brick-built changing room could be constructed as part of, or to include in some way, the plant house, where the filtration systems and the pumps for the pool are installed.

As electricity will need to be installed to run the pumps and machines, there will be little extra expense to add a shower for washing after swimming. As a shower room is a wet area, it should be tiled or decorated to withstand moisture. It may also be beneficial to install a toilet and a sink so that even those people who are not swimming but who are socializing on the patio can use the adjacent facilities without the inconvenience of having to make their way back to the main house.

A pool house is also a good way of keeping damp and dirt out of the main house. If small children are swimming and then playing in a sandbox or on a lawn, they can be washed and dried before going indoors. You can also use the pool house as an annex to a barbecue patio and have a fridge to keep drinks and food cool, and possibly a cabinet for utensils as well as a sink for washing up. China, flatware, glasses, and items used around the pool can be stored there, cutting down on the amount of fetching and carrying required whenever you want to use the pool.

With these cabin or poolhouse facilities, it is very important to ensure that all pipes and cables are well insulated against cold weather and whenever the facilities are not being used for several months; otherwise, the pipes may freeze and burst.

Wooden constructions are also a useful addition to a poolside, but should be erected on a concrete or similarly permanent and firm base. Gazebos with open sides are a good way of providing shelter over a dining area and can be equipped with rolldown canvas panels to give more privacy and shade when needed.

OPPOSITE, LEFT A Roman temple–style pool house stands regally at the foot of an appropriately classically shaped pool. The temple's ample curtains can be closed for extra shade or changing space, but can be taken down, washed, and stored between seasons.

OPPOSITE, RIGHT This deck area can be wholly open to the pool and landscape or shaded by long curtains that can be drawn in a number of ways.

ABOVE An old shed or unused storage facility can be converted into a pool house. Part may be used to store the pump and necessary machinery while the rest could contain a fridge for cool drinks and a shower.

RIGHT A shower plumbed through the outside wall of a house is an ideal place to rinse off after a swim or to enjoy a cooling shower. If you install a shower in such a location, make sure the water can be turned off to prevent pipes from bursting during periods of low temperatures.

ABOVE A freestanding wall, painted in a contrasting color to the main building, contains a stationary and a hand-held showerhead. The hand-held shower is useful for hosing off the soles of your feet or for directing a more powerful spray at a particular area.

TOP RIGHT The tank on the top of the four supporting legs is fed with water that can be turned on for a contained but adequate outdoor shower.

ABOVE RIGHT This shower area at the side of the pool makes use of the same waterproof floor and wall materials, but provides clean, chemical-free water to wash in.

OPPOSITE When showering outdoors, you don't need to be restricted by curtains or screens. Here, a small recess contains the excess water and directs it to a drain, and a movable ladder provides a handy place to hang a towel.

The seasonal or temporary option is a tent or canvas cabin, which can be set up for the summer when the pool or hot tub is most used then taken down and stored for the winter. Tents can be decorative and colorful or just simple green or beige canvas constructions; they will provide privacy in which to change and can also be a sunshade if the side flaps are rolled up.

A temporary but effective shower (albeit with cold water only), such as those used on camping trips, can be set up using a garden hose from an outdoor faucet or pumped through a simple wooden shower stall with a metal showerhead—these can be purchased from outdoor equipment suppliers.

Indoor changing areas can be a simple screen for undressing behind or a more elaborate set of rooms for drying, undressing, and storing clothes and beauty products, with chairs or benches for sitting and relaxing. The changing room should be decorated in a similar or compatible style to the main pool area; and good ventilation will be a priority to prevent any gym gear, clothing, towels, or mats from becoming damp and moldy.

furniture

Poolside furniture needs to be both waterproof and rustproof, with covers and cushions that are resistant to chemicals such as chlorine and those used in sun-protection creams. Furniture for outdoor use also needs to be weatherproof and upholstered or covered with fabrics that are not likely to bleach, fade, or rot when placed in regular contact with the sun.

There are many choices when it comes to furnishing poolside areas and patios, but a good guideline is to choose furniture that suits the style of your pool. For example, if you have a modern, urban glass and gray-tiled pool, look at contemporary furniture lines made with steel and spaghetti-like plastic lattice seats or molded plastic in the style of designers such as Vernor Panton and Phillipe Starck. If, on the other hand, your pool is in a more rural location surrounded by beds of shrubs and flowers, Lloyd Loom and rattan furniture or teak and treated pine seats and recliners would be more appropriate.

You may also want to divide the furnishings between the immediate poolside and the general pool area. Chairs and lounges used directly beside the pool need to be most water resistant, suitable for people in wet swimwear, and less durable furniture is placed in a secondary zone used by nonswimmers.

OPPOSITE, TOP This modern round seat accommodates a couple sitting together or a single person sunbathing, and the footstools that double as tables are also useful. The seat covers can be removed for cleaning, an important feature for furniture that comes into contact with fruit drinks, sun lotions, and preparations.

OPPOSITE, BOTTOM LEFT Built-in furniture is usually sturdy and weatherproof, staying poolside all year round. A wide bench such as this can be used as a seat, table, or recliner, depending on your needs.

OPPOSITE, BOTTOM RIGHT Metal is commonly used for outdoor furniture. It should be finished with rustproof paint and softened with cushions for prolonged periods of use.

BELOW Traditional rattan tables and chairs made from natural fibers such as palm leaves or bamboo is lightweight and easy to move around, but should not be left outdoors all year round.

BELOW RIGHT Adjustable recliners are a traditional pool-side furnishing; the head can be raised to make reading or drinking easy or let down to a flat surface for sunbathing.

BOTTOM RIGHT Poolside furniture should be comfortable for reclining or sitting in a swimsuit, so padded cushions are a welcome addition to any chair or lounge.

Some of the most practical seating can be built into low walls or surrounds; these can be constructed as the wall is being built, or can be added later to abut the wall, using it as a back plate or support. This built-in furniture will be in position all year round, but its weather-beaten appearance can be refreshed annually with a coat of paint.

The hard surfaces may also be softened with cushions that are brought out in the morning and stored indoors in the evening. A long stone bench is a good feature; it can be used to seat a couple of people, as a day bed by one, or even a table with portable chairs arranged around it.

A built-in barbecue or cooking area with food preparation stations on either side can be constructed as part of a whole cement, brick, or stone entertainment space, including some benches. A permanent outdoor grill may be erected as part of a hearth, with an overhead chimney to help draw the flame and duct the smoke away from the chef.

Another feature around which people like to gather is a fire pit. This can be a simple ring of stones encircling a fire, a more sophisticated hearthlike arrangement with a grid and stand for a pot, kettle, or grilling rack, or a sophisticated all-purpose case and stand, which contains the fire.

A hot tub can successfully be incorporated into a deck area, with the tub set in one corner and built-in wooden benches and seating areas on either side. If a barbecue is

part of the arrangement, it is best located as far away from the tub as possible, so that there is no danger of hot coals or spitting fat coming in contact with the tub or its users.

Molded plastic is frequently used for outdoor furniture because it is not initially affected by weather or rain—the main disadvantage is that it can be sweaty to sit or lie on for prolonged periods, especially in the heat. It is easily maintained with a soft brush, a little detergent, and a hose-down with water, but it will, if exposed to year-round weather conditions, become brittle and may discolor or even crack over time.

Wood is a classic material for outdoor furniture; teak, nyatoh, and pine are widely used. Wood is a comfortable natural material to sit on—though it may need softening with a cushion or pad; it is hardy and will survive all year round in the outdoors, although regular maintenance with varnish or oil is necessary to preserve it.

Metal furniture is usually painted or finished with a seal or coating to prevent it from becoming rusty, especially cast iron, which is used for ornate Victorian-style furniture. Another period of metal furniture is inspired by French café style. Lightweight tubular steel is not as prone to rust or water damage as iron; it provides a sturdy frame for many types of outdoor seating.

It is advisable to keep the area around the pool and hot tub as clutter free as possible, making it safer to move around and giving easy access to the water, so having some foldaway and stackable furniture can be useful. There are also times when there might be only a few people using the facilities, but others, such as at a family party or an afternoon with friends and neighbors, when more seating is necessary, so chairs can be brought out of storage and used but returned when no longer needed. Certain designs of polypropylene and plastic chairs, as well as some with metal frames, are designed with this in mind.

The classic director's chair and traditional wood-framed deck chair are also practical and have the advantage that if their canvas covers wear, rip, or become damaged, they can easily be replaced. The cotton canvas covers are also comfortable to sit on because the fabric breathes and is therefore not sweaty.

Lounges come in a range of shapes and materials; the classic teak recliner or steamer chair is appropriate in most locations and some have a detachable footrest, which can also double as a stool or side table. The back is usually adjustable—this is an asset since you can put the back into an upright position to read comfortably but lie it down flat to sunbathe.

In fully equipped entertaining spaces there may be a kitchen or island unit or even a bar, and to sit comfortably at this raised level you will need a high stool. An appropriate stool will have a foot rung so your feet have something to rest on, and an area of back support. If the stools do not have a rung, you may consider putting a foot rail along the facing of the island unit to provide a general footrest. If a stool doesn't have a back support, people tend to lean forward and slump over the bar top.

Hanging furniture such as hammocks and wicker tub or bowl chairs can be suspended from a sturdy branch or a specifically designed metal support. The base of the metal support should be firmly secured to a deck or surface area so that it doesn't topple over, and you should test the strength of a branch or trunk before going to the effort of tying up the ropes for a hammock or seat.

Tables are available from large-scale dining to small occasional size. A small stool or table by a lounge is useful for holding sunglasses, magazines, a drink, and sun lotion, keeping these items off a damp poolside or out of the way of pets and insects. Larger tables, especially those that can be extended to increase the number of settings, are ideal for patio or pergola dining areas. If the table is not to be used under a permanent shade, it is useful to find one with a hole in the center so that a sun umbrella can be slotted through to provide direct shade above the table top. Tables can be purchased in a number of different materials, from plastic to wood, and they may be covered with a cloth or dressed with mats for a more decorative or formal appearance.

To transport food from the house to the al fresco dining area, barbecue, or poolside, a cart is useful. You can transport a lot in one journey, saving several trips back and forth.

If you don't have enough storage space indoors, you may need to cover some of the bulkier pieces of furniture, such as benches and barbecues, with waterproof covers during the winter. These covers can be bought from garden furniture suppliers.

OPPOSITE, LEFT Adjustable and adaptable furniture is the key to successful outdoor living. This trio of wooden benches can be arranged as a poolside seat—here they follow the outline of the pool edge—or divided into three separate seats or small side tables. They could also be used to stack towels or to support a tray of drinks.

OPPOSITE, RIGHT Outdoor hearths and fire pits are a way of prolonging the use of poolside areas, whether into the cool of the evening, after sunset, or at times of the year when the sun is not at full strength. The traditional fire pit was just a hole in the ground ringed with large rocks, but the modern interpretation is more sophisticated and includes steel and metal containers with internal grids on a raised base.

ABOVE This barbecue features a metal grille suspended over a raised charcoal burner. The heat source is elevated so it doesn't damage the wood of the deck area, and the swinging grill makes it easy to pull the cooking food away from the direct heat source if it needs to be turned or removed. With metal grilles and open fires it is important to remember that the metal itself heats up and should be approached with care when you are dressed only in swimwear or lightweight clothes.

RIGHT Solid wooden garden furniture is usually weather resistant and can be left outdoors all year round, though direct sun may cause the depth of color to fade. The wood should be treated annually to maintain its durability, and it can be stained to revive its color.

shades and awnings

Enoying the outdoor life is about having the right quantities of light and shade. There are certain times of the day, when the sun is directly overhead and at its strongest, when it is best to be in the shade; and for those with delicate skin, such as young children and the elderly, a little sunshine can go a long way. So providing areas of shade should always be considered when planning an outdoor area. Trees and shrubs can provide an effective and attractive natural barrier from the rays of the sun. The broad leafy branches of a mature tree are ideal, as are the fronds and branches of more tropical blooms, such as palms and bamboo.

The traditional umbrella or store-window awning that pulls out from a wall above a doorway will also give shelter, but there are some more interesting contemporary designs that take inspiration from yacht sails and tepees. These canvas or Kevlar (Kevlar is a sturdy weatherproof material used for sails) panels are held in place with high-tension steel yacht rigging and steel poles; the canvas can also be punched with metal eyelets that are threaded through with cord or rope and then lashed to a pole or frame.

Sun umbrellas have the undoubted advantage of being comparatively lightweight and portable; they can be moved

OPPOSITE, TOP This lightweight but permanent sun screen shades a dining table without obscuring the view.

OPPOSITE, BOTTOM Canvas and similar sturdy fabrics can be used for tentlike awnings.

ABOVE LEFT Slatted screens offer dappled shade while still allowing air to circulate.

ABOVE Light and shade are important in exposed positions where natural cover is scarce.

LEFT This cantilevered shade provides protection from the sun, but its lightweight construction lets the light pass through.

BELOW LEFT A simple roof canopy will provide protection when the sun is directly above.

around as the sun travels across the sky, so that the maximum cover is always available. Some large umbrellas can be anchored firmly into a base; these can be either a steel base plate and socket that is screwed to the deck or ground surface, or a plastic base filled with either water or gravel. Some of the modern garden umbrellas come with an adjustable arm so that they project at right angles to the base and do not need the pole or support to be in the center of a seating area or table.

Because it is sometimes bright but not very warm, or if the evening chill closes in after a day of sunshine, there are a number of outdoor heaters on the market that run mainly on canister or bottled gas. These heaters have moved from the commercial realms of sidewalk cafés to the home poolside and can extend the seasonal as well as nighttime use of an outdoor area.

walls and screens

Screening an outdoor pool or hot tub area is often necessary in an urban setting; it can help reduce the noise factor as well as giving a feeling of privacy. In a larger rural spot, walls and hedges can be a useful windbreak as well. Lattice and trellis partitions are both decorative and practical. Their open composition allows the wind to blow through, so in windy areas they are ideal because they put up little resistance but can be covered with climbing plants and flowers to give some protection. In a similar location a solid fence could be blown down by a strong gust.

Brick and concrete block walls can appear hard and plain, but if they are plastered and painted, they can become a more integral part of the landscape or the pool area. It is best to avoid a pure white finish because in brilliant sunlight it will reflect the light and produce glare that is hard on the eyes. The wall can be painted a color that complements the main house if it is within view, surrounding vegetation, or the interior of the hot tub or pool; or it can be used as a support for decorative or scented plants such as bougainvillea, clematis, or honeysuckle.

Walls and screens with gates are also an important safety feature as they can encircle and enclose a pool and ensure that access by young children and animals is achieved only under

ABOVE LEFT A wall can be used to screen and contain a pool, to give privacy, and also to protect an exposed location from extremes of weather.

ABOVE RIGHT A mosaic panel makes a plain wall into a more decorative feature; a mural can also be used to the same effect.

OPPOSITE A military-style camouflage screen has been suspended in front of a plain wall to give the impression that it is covered with climbing plants. The screen is hung like a curtain so it can be pulled back or replaced to give a different appearance and ambience to the pool surround.

appropriate adult supervision. The most widely used material for this purpose is fine metal mesh screens set on metal posts that are embedded in concrete. A locking gate that can be opened either with a key or a security panel controls entry.

For an indoor pool or hot tub enclosed by a conservatory or glass extension, the problem of being overlooked can be resolved by installing opaque glass or silver-coated one-way glass, which allows the person inside to look out while the person on the outside sees only a mirrored panel. Blinds, especially the louvered variety, can also be tilted so there is access for natural light but the view is obscured for anyone looking in.

It is best to avoid using yards of curtains or awnings as the material will absorb moisture and might start to rot over time. Also, unless treated to be resistant, colors and patterns will bleach and fade rapidly in direct sunlight, although there are some specially formulated modern dyes that have greater staying power, and they are used specifically for outdoor fabrics.

ABOVE LEFT A fine wooden slat wall encloses a pool area and makes it secluded, but it isn't restrictive; wind and air can still circulate freely, and the natural color of the screen makes it blend in with its surroundings.

LEFT This curving stone wall links the pool to the garden around it; the uneven surface and varying colors give it a rugged, grottolike appearance.

ABOVE Hedges can be grown and shaped to create walls and surrounds to pools, but opt for an evergreen such as yew. The yew hedge is dense, but not as likely to shed leaves as beech or other deciduous plants.

OPPOSITE In an indoor pool the wall surfaces are the largest overall decorative feature. They can be paneled or painted to establish or endorse a design.

LEFT A diving board should be firmly anchored in concrete at the poolside or through the deck, and it must be maintained in perfect condition, with an antislip cover and no signs of cracking or warping.

BELOW A diving board must only be positioned at the deepest end of the pool, and it is unwise to dive into the shallow end, even from the poolside.

slides and boards

Slides and diving boards are only suitable for use with certain sizes and depths of pools, and you must check that your pool can accommodate them safely. The guidelines are that for a standard 6ft long by 18in wide (1.8m by 45cm) board, the pool must be at least 8½ft (2.6m) deep, 15ft (4.5m) wide, and 28ft (8.5m) long. The board should be positioned at the deep end of the pool and the base set firmly in concrete. To avoid accidents the surface of the board and the surrounding area should be slip resistant.

Slides are usually made of fiberglass or steel and can be straight or with a slight curve or bend at the water end. The curve is useful in a pool that isn't very wide because the slide user will come off to one side rather than directly into the center of the water. Slides often have an integral set of steps, and there should also be rails on each side to aid the person ascending.

Another option is a diving rock or group of rocks. These are specifically made to give a natural appearance to a pool edge, and the rock is set into the surround so that about a third of it hangs over the water, while the rest is set on dry land.

ladders, rails, and steps

Preformed step units give a gradual entry into the pool water and also provide a sitting or resting shelf. This sort of access is ideal if the pool is used by very young or elderly swimmers because the wide step and gradual submersion makes it easier and less hazardous to enter the water. These types of steps can be made as an integral part of a fiberglass cast or constructed from concrete or blocks as the foundation of the pool is made. The steps can be positioned in the center of the pool, fanning out from a corner or square on to a corner, and their size and location will be governed by the shape and capacity of the pool.

Hot tubs don't usually have steps per se but may have a series of graduated internal levels on which you can step down and also use as a bench on which to sit or lie. These levels are preformed in the fiberglass or acrylic tub shells, or incorporated during the building process if the tub is cast in concrete.

A tread ladder is another way of getting in and out of a pool, and may be required for access to an above-ground hot tub. Tread ladders are usually precast in stainless steel and secured to the wall of the pool underwater and the deck or surround above water. The treads of these steps should be ribbed or covered with a rubber nonslip finish to make sure wet feet make good and secure contact with them. Any ladder or rails must be set or mounted securely, and there should be no sharp edges, bolts, or screw heads left sticking up. In a wide or long pool it may be necessary to have two ladders or a set of steps at one end and a ladder at the other. The lower step of the ladder need not be on the floor of the pool, but it should be positioned so that the bottom step is easy to reach by both children and adults.

ABOVE Safe entry and exit is paramount; the combination of well-positioned rails and ladders or steps achieve this. A metal rail and integral ladder are popular in sunken or recessed pools, and they are designed so that the span of the rail and the incline of the step correspond.

RIGHT A vertical ladder-and-rail combination gives direct access into the deep end of an eco pool.

FAR RIGHT The upper surface of the steps in this style of ladder system should be ribbed or textured to make sure wet feet get a good firm grip on them.

ABOVE These steps link a pool and deck area to an elevated changing cabin. For safety, the sides of the rails have been filled in with regularly spaced steel cable that would support someone if he or she happened to slip on the way in or out.

RIGHT A long, gradually stepped pool entry with corresponding rails is ideal for families with young children; adults will want to enter the water slowly and carefully while supervizing junior swimmers. This arrangement works equally well for older adults, who might find it difficult to cope with the acute angle of a traditional steep ladder.

ABOVE LEFT Integral steps molded in the poured concrete base of a pool can be covered with the same tiles or finish as the main pool. Here the steps are designed to fan out around the base of the hot tub; they can be used to access the pool both from the tub and the poolside.

ABOVE RIGHT Following the contours of the rounded section of the pool, these wide, shallow steps double as submerged seats and make an interesting visual underwater pool feature.

LEFT The surfaces of tiled steps should be regularly washed with a stiff bristle brush to prevent them from becoming slippery with excess sun oil, garden debris, or algae. The tread of steps with no handrails must be wide enough to accommodate an adult foot and should be gently sloping, not steep.

OPPOSITE The low, flat steps into this pool are between the wall of an integral hot tub and a section of deck, so the low walls act as a support for people getting in or out of the water.

pool and tub covers

Covers are an effective way of saving on operating costs and can be installed for both indoor and outdoor pools and tubs. Effective covers act as a seal over the water surface, keeping heat loss to a minimum. When the cover is in place, the surrounding air can be allowed to fall to a temperature below that of the pool or tub water without any adverse effects. But before the cover is removed on an indoor pool, air temperature should be raised to normal levels.

A well-fitting cover will also reduce the amount of evaporation from the water surface and, for outdoor pools and tubs, prevent leaves and debris from entering. Tub covers are usually a thick insulated pad in a waterproof casing that can be held in place over the top of the tub by sturdy snaps or interlocking clasps sited around the edge of the cover and the outer lip or rim of the tub.

Pool covers, especially the articulated, plastic panel variety that rest on a ledge above the waterline, can create an almost solid, floorlike top, that will prevent young children or animals from entering the water and hold them safely above it if they should trip or fall over the pool surround.

A pool cover can be a retractable articulated panel that is drawn out from its storage area at the end of the pool and, like a horizontal garage door, brought along the length of the pool. This type of cover is built during the construction stage, but if you are adding a cover retrospectively, a floating padded panel, stored on an automated roller, is an option. Once turned on, the roller will automatically roll up the cover ready for the pool to be used.

Some pool and tub covers have a metallic inner surface that helps reflect heat back into the water, and others contain a thick insulation layer that has a similar effect. Covers should not be stored damp for long periods because the fabric can become moldy. If this happens, the surface should be washed with a mild solution of detergent and left to dry thoroughly.

TOP ROW This cover works on an elevator mechanism, which lowers it to the pool base when the water is being used but raises it to look like a part of the driveway or patio area when it is not in use.

OPPOSITE, BOTTOM RIGHT Pool covers can be built into the rim support at the side of the pool so they don't require separate storage.

OPPOSITE BOTTOM LEFT Pool covers can be tailor-made to suit any free-form shape or combination of pool and hot tub. They can also be remotely operated so the cover will extend and retract without any physical intervention.

RIGHT If adult supervision is not available for children in the pool area, make sure the cover is securely in place. The cover, if compliant with safety standards, will support a child's weight, should one accidentally fall on it.

safety and health

Safety must be your number-one priority around a pool or tub area; surfaces are hard and may be slippery, so any fall or bump can result in severe bruising, and worse, a break or concussion. Overexercising or tiredness can lead to cramps and spasms, which may make it difficult to reach the pool edge or the shallow end, so a life guard or competent adult, not in the pool, should be on watch. Adults swimming or exercising alone should notify another member of the household that they are doing so, and no child should be near a pool without supervision. The adult supervising or someone within the family group should have basic first aid and resuscitation training. There should also be a first-aid kit on hand, a telephone nearby, and a life preserver or rescue pole with a flexible loop end kept at the water's edge.

In the construction of a heated pool, Jacuzzi, or hot tub, there is the potential for electricity and water to meet; this lethal combination must be avoided at all costs, so the installation must be done using only recommended materials and by a qualified professional with expertise in pool building. All filters and vents should be protected with adequate guards to prevent mechanisms from coming in contact with clothing, fingers, toes or hair.

Child- and animal-proof fences and pool covers are also useful; not only do they effectively shut off or seal the surface of the pool, keeping the water safely away from direct contact with children, but the cover will also help to keep the water clean and conserve heat. Laws in many places now require alarms, fencing, or covers for all private swimming pools to prevent unaccompanied children from accessing or playing around the pool and to guard against them tripping or falling into the water and drowning; and this is a useful precaution in any area.

Getting in and out of the water may be difficult or frightening for small children, the elderly, or those with walking difficulties, but a gently sloping beach-type entrance will make access easier. Rails or handles on the sides of steps are also beneficial, as are gently graduated steps rather than a steep ladder.

If the pool is to be used by children, it is advisable to have a graduated base or two-level pool, with one end shallow and the other deeper for an adult swimming and diving. The shallow end will prevent children from feeling intimidated by the depth of water and will also allow an adult to stand comfortably and securely beside a child while supervising his or her swimming.

The health aspects of pools and hot tubs are also important. A swimmer is only lightly clothed, so ambient and pool temperatures should be comfortably warm, especially for pools used by small children or the elderly who feel the cold more acutely than an active adult. Swimmers who remain in wet swimsuits in a cool environment may be vulnerable to chills; also the body temperature will decrease after activity, so it is best to leave the pool, wash, dry, and change, or lie in the sun. Small children may protest at leaving the pool even though they are shivering, but they will be vulnerable to colds and illness if their body temperature drops significantly. A brisk rubdown with a towel will improve warmth and circulation or a warm drink can help. Although swimming is a good exercise for those recovering from injury or with health problems such as arthritis, you should always check with your doctor that you are physically fit enough to cope with this sort of activity.

Be careful when choosing a pool-maintenance system because some chemicals can irritate the eyes, causing them to become bloodshot. People with sensitive skin, allergies, or complaints such as eczema may also find that regular or prolonged swimming in water treated with a high dose of chemicals can exacerbate their problems; and if the skin is cut or cracked, saline cleaning solutions can cause a certain amount of stinging.

Breathing problems can be affected by the chemicals in a pool, especially indoor pools where the chemical vapor lies above the surface of the warm water in the zone where you breathe in the air during exercising. Effective ventilation and use of nonchemical water purifiers can eliminate this problem.

Hygiene is extremely important around pool and tub areas. Tiles and surfaces should be regularly washed and hosed down to prevent mold or bacterial buildup. Nonslip mats and filter grids should also be removed so that the area beneath them, as well as the items themselves, can be thoroughly cleaned. With bare feet there is the risk of the spread of skin problems such as fungal infections; a shallow antiseptic foot bath can help prevent this. With hot tubs and Jacuzzis, the filters, pipes, and drains must regularly be flushed through and treated with an antibacterial agent, because water that rests in the bends of the pipe or base of a mechanism may become stagnant or stale, which can encourage slime or bad-smelling and unpleasant algae to develop.

OPPOSITE A pool and hot tub can give much pleasure and enjoyment if used with care and caution. Just as electricity and water are a bad combination and should only be brought together by a qualified contractor, so are heat, water, and alcohol, so be especially careful if you are entertaining in and around a pool area. Maintenance is also vital to keep the water sparkling, clean, and inviting, and there are many products that can assist in making it an easy task.

ARCHITECTS AND DESIGNERS

ACQ
020 7491 4272
www.acq-architects.com

Piet Boon
Ambacht 6
1511 JZ Oostzaan
Netherlands
0031756843656
www.pietboon.nl

Clarke:Desai
10 Foundling Court
Marchmont Street
London WC1 1AN
020 7278 933
www.clarkedesai.com

Collett-Zarzycki
020 8969 69 67
www.collett-zarzycki.com

Bruno Erpicum and Partners
452 An Reine Astrid
B 1950 Kraainem
Belgium
0032 2 687 27 17
www.erpicum.org

Freedom Pools (Central Coast)
P/L, 417 Manns Rd
West Gosford
New South Wales
Australia 2250
Tel: (02) 4325 0813
Fax: (02) 4325 0821
Email:freedom@freedompools.com.au
www.freedompools.com.au

Peter Glass and Associates
Landscape Architects and
Pool Designers
Level 2, 69 Christie Street
St Leonards
NSW 2065
Australia.
61 2 9906 2727
www.peterglass.com.au

David Hallam Ltd
7 Brompton Road
Sheffield S9 2PA
0114 244 0013
www.davidhallamltd.co.uk

Holger Stewen
00 34 971 653312
www.holgerstewen.com

Patrick Mazure
Les Piscine Patrick Mazure
00 33 4 74 08 16 21
www.piscines-mazure.com

Pool Design
01666 840065
www.pool-design.co.uk

Manolo Mestre
00 1 52 555 596 9545

Michaelis Boyd Associates
90a Notting Hill Gate
London W11 3HP
020 7221 1237
www.michaelisboyd.com

Munckenbeck + Marshall
Architects
135 Curtain Road
London EC2H 3BX
020 7739 3300
and
45E 20th Street
4th Floor
New York 10003
001 212 982 8219
www.mandm.uk.com

Niall McLaughlin Architects
39-51 Highgate Road
London NW5 1RS
020 74859170
www.niallmclaughlin.com

Marmol Radziner and Associates
(USA)
12210 Nabraska Avenue
Los Angeles
CA 90025
310 826 6222
www.marmol-radziner.com

Oxford Pools
0845 8800766
www.oxfordpools.co.uk

Anthony Paul MSGD
Landscape Designer and Consultant
Black and White Cottage
Standon Lane
Ockley
Surrey RH5 5QR
01306 627677
www.anthonypaullandscapedesign.com

Powell Tuck Associates
6 Stamford Brook Road
London W6 0XH
020 8749 7700
www.powelltuck.co.uk

Rainbow Pools London Ltd
The Tannery
Queen Street
Gomshall
Surrey GU 5 9IY
0870 405 0567
www.rainbowpools.co.uk

Robin Ellis
020 7449 4252
www.robinellis.co.uk

Richard Paxton Architects
020 7586 6161
www.rparch.com

Paxton Locher
15b St Georges Mews
London SW1 8XE
020 75866161

Sills Huniford (USA)
001 212 988 1636
www.sillshuniford.com

Swaney Draper Architects (Australia)
376 Albert St
East Melbourne
Victoria 3002
Australia
00 61 9417 6162
mail@swaneydraper.com.au

Gunter Weidner
Planungsburo Gunter Weidner
Professor Schlosserstrasse 2
Kufstein
Austria
0043 5372 61018
weidnerplan@kufnet.at

Seth Stein
020 8968 8581
www.sethstein.com

Taylor Howes Designs
29 Fernshaw Road
London SW10 0TG
0207 349 9017
www.thdesigns.co.uk

Yves Zoccola
Les Bonfillions
13100 Satin-Marc-Jaumergarde
France
00 33 4 42 24 93 43
wwwdecopiscine.com

SUPPLIERS

GARDEN AND LANDSCAPE

Award Pools and Landscapes
PO Box 6763
Baulkham Hills Business Centre
New South Wales 2153
02 9629 3639
www.awardpools.com.au

Imagination Design Concepts
588 Perugia Way
Los Angeles
California 90077
310 471 5024
email thornbury@earthlink.net
tackle a wide range of architecturally
led design projects

Piet Oudolf
00 31 314 381 120
www.oudolf.com

Arne Maynard (Garden design)
Clerkenwell House
125 Golden Lane
London EC1Y 0TJ
020 7689 8100
www.arne-maynard.com

Natural Designs
3750 West Indian School Road
Phoenix
Arizona 05019
602 532 3700
www.shastapools.com

Michelle Osborne
(Landscape Consultant)
www.panoramalandscapes.com
The Parson's Garden
The Garden Room
30 Gladwin Road
Colchester
Essex CO2 7HS
01206 570 440
www.theparsonsgarden.co.uk

Scenic Landscaping
7 Argyle Street
Haskell
New Jersey 07420
973 616 9600
www.sceniclandscaping.com
Garden and landscape design

Steve Martino & Associates
3336 N 32nd Street, Suite 110
Phoenix
Arizona 85018
602 957 6150
www.stevemartino.net
Landscape and architectural design

NATURAL SWIMMING PONDS

Biotop Landschaftsgestaltung
Gesellschaft m.b.H
A-3400 Klosterneuburg -Weidling
Haupstrasse 285
02243 304 06
www.swimming-teich.com

Jurgen McClananhan
Fuchs baut Garten GbbH
Schlegldorf 91a, 83661
Lenggries
0176 20 888 220 or 08042
914540
www.fuchs-baut-garten.de

Garten Art
020 7239 8294
wwwgartenart.co.uk

Michael Littlewood
01460 240168
www.ecodesign.co.uk

L'Eau Naturel
01223 290029
www.garden-landscape.com

HOT TUBS AND ENDLESS POOLS

Clearwater Spas
2 Encon Court
Owl Close
Moulton Park
Industrial Estate,
Northampton NN3 6HZ
01604 670 898
www.clearwaterspas.co.uk

Endless Pools, Inc.
www.endlesspools.co.uk
0800 028 1056 ext. 4736
200 E. Dutton Mill Road
Aston
PA 19014
All Endless Pool components fit through a standard doorway or down stairs making installation possible in existing spaces like a basement or garage

Hot Spring Garden Spas
and Hot Tubs
The Spa Showrooms
41 Robjohns Rd
Chelmsford
Essex CM1 3AG
01245 265036
branches in Manchester, Reading, Bristol, Reigate and Warwick
free phone 0800 085888
www.hotspring.co.uk

Jacuzzi
01782 718002
www.jacuzzi.co.uk

Kissel GmbH
Heizungen Bäder Schwimmbäder
Klima Photovoltaik
Mercedesstrasse 6
71139 Ehningen
07034/9370-0
www.kissel.de

Nordic
01883 732 400
www.noprdic.co.uk

Spa Connection
77a Station Road
Ratho Station
Edinburgh EH28 8QP
087 240 7650
www.spaconnection.co.uk

SwimEx
020 8749 3343
www.swimex.com

Terete Hot Tubs
01609 883 103
www.teretehottubs.co.uk

POOL INSTALLATION AND MAINTAINANCE

Swimming Pool & Allied Trades
Association (SPATA)
01264 356210
www.spata.co.uk
Advice body and source directory

Azure Leisure Industries
01276 475566

Buckingham Pools
01926852351
www.buckinghampools.com

E+M Technica
Mechanical and electrical services
01784 431333

Fibre Co
Green Farm House
The Pike
Washington
West Sussex RH20 4AA
01903 891558
www.fibre-co.com

Guncast Pools
08702 410736
www.guncast.com

London Swimming Pool Company
020 8874 0414
www.londonswimmingpools.com

Penguin Swimming Pools
016 833327
www.penguinpools.co.uk

Rutherford The Pool People
01424 775060
www.applegate.co.uk

POOL ACCESSORIES

FURNITURE

Breeze House
Sunnyhills Road
Barnfields, Lee
Staffordshire ST13 5RJ
01538 398 488
www.breezehouse.co.uk
open-sided timber buildings for outdoor entertaining

The Collection & Teak Direct
The Old Grain Barn
Lower Cultham Farm
Black Boys Lane
Henly-on-Thames
Oxon RG9 3DP
www.theakdiect.co.uk

Conmoto
The Pool Room
Stanstead House
Stanstead Park
Rowlands Castle
Hants PO9 6DX
02392 410045
www.encompassco.com
Stylish weatherproof furniture and accessories

Cyan
Unit 6
Coulsdon North Industrial Estate
Station Approach
Coulsdon,
Surrey CR5 2NR
08456 789 890
www.cyan-teak-furniutre.com
traditional and contemporary garden and leisure furniture

The Cotswold Garden Company
101 Northwick Business Park
Blockley
Moreton-in-March
Gloucestershire GL54 5JE
01386 700 753
www.cotswold-garden.com
maintenance free aluminium garden furniture

Dedon furniture
Zeppelinstraße 22, 21337
Lüneburg
Germany
041 31 / 22 44 70
Fax: 041 31 / 22 447 30
E-mail: office@dedon.de

Gloster Furniture Ltd,
Concorde Road
Patchway
Bristol BS34 5TB
01179315335
www.gloster.com
Contemporary teak and rattan furniture, cushions and parasols

Habitat
08456 010740
www.habitat.com

Indian Ocean
0870 780 4476
www.indian-ocean.co.uk

Lloyd Loom Furniture
3/13 Chelsea Harbour Design Centre
London SW10 OXE
020 7352 2312
www.vincentsheppard.com

Marks and Spencers
www.marksandspencer.com
Furniture and accessories

Pangea Home
53 Lambs Conduit Street
London WC1N 3NB
020 7404 9179
www.pangeahome.com
stylish contemporary loungers and tables

The Pavilion
www.teakpavilion.com
a raised teak finish pavilion with deck and railings

Phileas Frog
31 Weald Hall Farm
Canes Lane
Essex CM16 6ND
01992577422
www.phileasfrog.co.uk

Reflex
Via Paris Bordone 82
1-31030 Biancade
Treviso
Italy
00 39 0422 844430
www.reflexangeloc.com
furniture and specialist glass and glass manufacturers

Teak Tiger
Crestland House
Bull Lande Ind Estate
Sudbury
Suffolk CO10 OBD
01787 880900
www.teaktiger.com

Trout Studios
2727 11th Street
Santa Monica
California 90405
512 894 0774
www.troutstudios.com
Outdoor furniture, cast aluminium tiles and architectural design

Vitra
30 Clerkenwell Road
London EC1M 5PG
020 76086200
www.vitra.com

BLINDS AND AWNINGS

Appeal
0800 975 5757
www.appealblinds.com
Fabric, French Pinoleum and Solar R blinds

Luxaflex
0800 652 7799
www.luxaflex.com
wide range of manual and electronically controlled awnings and shades, wind sensors available, made in solution-dyed acrylic and PVC fabrics

Gandia Blasco
www.gandiablasco.com
modern shades and porticos

Thomas Sanderson
0800 220 603
www.thomassanderson.com
a wide range of traditional and contemporary screens and awnings

Regal Awnings
101 Crow Green Road
Pilgrims Hatch
Brentwood
Essex CM15 9RP
01708 502 669
www.regalwnings.co.uk
Dutch canopies and awnings in over 300 fabrics

I-D Systems
Diamond Road
Norwich
Norfolk NR6 6NN
01603 408 804
www.i-d-systems co.uk
Folding doors in aluminum and timber

Sunfold Systems
The Greenhouse
93 Norwich Road
East Dereham
Norfolk NR20 3AL
01362 699 744
www.sunfoldsystems.co.uk
Folding and sliding doors, laminates and frameless doors

MOVABLE FLOORS

Aqualift
00 33 6 17 73 61 63
www.aqualift.fr

GP Construct
00 32 3 644 44 50
www.gpconstruct.be

POOL COVERS AND SHELTERS

Endless Summer Pool Enclosures
24 Queen Emma's
Witney
Oxford
01993 775227
www.pool-encolusres.co.uk/endless-summer

Eureka
00 33 3 8807 24 10
www.abri-eureka.com

Paridiso Kunden Centre
00 49 7807 925 825
www.paridso-international.com

Sun Abris
00 33 4 67 98 43 37
www.sun-abris.fr

Voeroka.GmbH
Gewerbestr. 4-6
D - 75031 Eppingen
07262 8087
Fax: 0 7262 123
info@voeroka.de

HEAT PUMPS, CLEANING AGENTS, AND DEHUMIDIFIERS

Univar Ltd
Lakeside
Cheadle Royal Business Park
Cheadle
Cheshire SK8 3GR
0161 741 7080
www.univar.co.uk
a comprehensive range of chlorine and sanitation products including the non chlorine cleaner Blue Crystal

Calorex Heat Pumps Ltd
The Causeway
Maldon
Essex CM9 5PU
01621 856611
www.calorex.com,
heat exchange and ventilation units

Clevaquip Pty Ltd
163-65 Greens Road
Dandenong South
Victoria 3195
phone (617) 3899 1877
www.cleva.com.au
Pool cleaning, salt chlorinators, pumps and filter systems

Pahlen
0046859411050
www.pahlen.com
water monitoring, dosing and quality-regulation systems

Pool-Water Products
6 Trade Place
Victoria 3133
03 9873 5055
www.poolwaterproducts.com.au

Recotherm Ltd.
1437 Pershore Road
Stirchley
Birmingham B30 2JL
0121 433 3622
www.recotherm.co.uk
Specialists in environmental control systems for indoor swimming pool

Simplee Solar
258 Woolsbridge Industrial Estate
Three Legged Cross
Wimbourn
Dorset BH21 6SP
01202 828 264
www.simpleesolar.co.uk
Solar water heating using hi-tech German technology

Triogen
0141 810 4861
ozone generators

FLOORING, DECKING, AND SURROUNDS

Burlingstone Stone
01229 889661
www.burlingstonestone.co.uk
specialists in Lake District slate and natural stone finishes

Dallmet Ltd
7 Constable Court
Lavenham
Suffolk CO10 9RB
017 87 248244
www.dallmer.de
Tinaflex rubber matting

Emco Hygine Emco UK
Suite 4.01
Grosvenor House
Central Park
Telford TF2 9TW
01952 200965
www.emco-bau.de
Mats and drain and overflow gratings

Euroglass Australia
showrooms in Brisbane and Gold Coast
1300 654 856
www.euroglass.com.au
Glass panels and frameless pool fencing

Island Stone
78 York St
London W1H 1DP
0800 083 9351
www.islandstone.co.uk
rounded pebble and originator of the mesh back pebble tile

Mandarin
01600 715444
www.mandarinstone.com
Natural Stone Floors and wall coverings, branches in Monmouth, Bath, Cheltenham and Cardiff

Nature Fushion
020 7627 5577

The Original Decking Company
www.original decking.co.uk
0800 587 4985

Original Stone Company
100–105 Victoria Crescent
Burton on Trent
Staffordshire DE14 2QF
01283 501090

The Orkney Stone Company Ltd
Church Road Street
Margarets Hope
Orkney KW17 2SR
01856 831 462
hand quarried, hand-split, hand dressed local stone

Slate World
Green World
97 Tomiano Avenue
London NW5 2RX
020 8204 3444
www.slateworld.com

Stone Age
Unit 3 Parsons Green Lane
London SW6 4HH
020 7384 9090
www.estone.co.uk-
over 30 types of sandstone and limestone

Stonehouse Tiles
45 Enterprise Business Estate
Balina Road
London SE16 3LF
020 7237 5375
www.stonehousetiles.co.uk

Stonell
521-525
Battersea Park Road
London SW11 3BN
020 7738 0606
www.stonelldirect.com - flag and stone tiles

TILES AND FINISHES

Bisazza
Unit 18 Boundary Business Court
92-94 Church Road
Mitcham,
Surrey CR4 3TD 020 8640 7994
www.bisazza.com

Glassflake
paint finish with glass flakes from Epoxyman Industrial Coatings, South Africa
27 33 3920062
www.lin-a-pool.com

House of Mosaics
Longbarn Village
Alceaster Heath
Alcester
Warwickshire B49 5JJ
010789 765000
www.houseofmosiacs.co.uk
glass and marble mosaics

Mosaic Design Company
235 The Boulevarde
Miranda
New South Wales 2228
phone (02) 954 1399
www.mosaic-design.com.au.
Imaginative and colourful mosaic designs

Opus Mosaics
120 Fore Street
Exeter EX43JQ
01392 496393
www.mosaicsbymailorder.co.uk

Stone 4 Less,
020 8748 8045
www.stone4less.com
natural stone mosaics

Worlds End Tiles
Railway Gardens Yard
Silverthorne Road
London SW8
0207 720 8358
www.worldsendtiles.co.uk
wide range of ceramic tiles, mat and shiny glaze, custom design service available

INDEX

Figures in italics indicate captions.

PICTURE CREDITS

Picture Research: Emily Hedges and David Penrose

The publisher would like to thank the following sources for their kind permission to reproduce the photographs in this book:

Page 1 Andrew Wood/Seth Stein; Andrew Wood/ Johann Slee; 3 Garden Picture Library/Ron Sutherland; 4-5 Ray Main/Powell Tuck Associates/Deepwater; 6-7 Ray Main/Georg Riedel/Gunther Weidner; 8 Andrew Wood/ Zarzycki; 9 Andrew Wood/Zarzycki/Garden design by Jean Mus; 10 The Interior Archive/Mark Luscombe-Whyte/Antti Louag; 11 The Interior Archive/Simon Upton/Anthony Collett; 12 Dedon/Christophe Dugied, Paris; 14-15 Trevor Mein/Swaney Draper; 16-17 Garden Picture Library; 18-19 Ray Main/Powell Tuck Associates/Deepwater; 19 inset l Ray Main/Munkenbeck and Marshall; 19 inset c Simon Upton/a house in Provence designed by Jean-Louis Raynaud and Kenyon Kramer and inset r Andrew Wood/Gandia Blasco/Ramon Esteve; 20 Stellan Herner/Skarp Agent AB; 22 tl and tr Rainbow Pools; 23 tr David Hallam Ltd; 23 tl Gerald Zugmann/The Next Enterprise; 23 b Edmund Sumner/VIEW; 24-27 Sarkis Boyadjian/Bobby Desai; 28 tl Pools and Spas; 28 top right Jean-Francois Jaussaud/Luxproductions; 28 b Pools and Spas; 29 David Hallam Ltd; 30-31 Ray Main/Mainstream Images; 32 l The Interior Archive/Luke White /Alberta Ferretti; 32-33 The Interior Archive/Andrew Wood/Gora Kodan Hotel,Japan; 34 Ray Main/Mainstream Images; 35 t and b David Grey; 36 t Rainbow Pools; 36 b Dennis Gilbert/VIEW; 37 tl Arcaid/Nicholas Kane/Belsize Architects; 37 tr and b Rainbow Pools; 38-41 Ray Main/Powell Tuck Associates/Deepwater; 42 Poolside Magazine/Sally Grainger/Neptune Pools; 44 and 45 t Arcaid/Alan Weintraub/John Lautner; 45 Andrew Wood/Helena Aruhente of Lautner Associates; 46–49 Ray Main/Munkenbeck and Marshall; 50-51 Voeroka; 52 Phil Aynsley Photography; 54 l Arcaid/Denton Corker Marshall; 54 r Terence Moore/Ronchetti Design; 55 Andrew Wood/Steven Ehrlich Architects; 55 tl and b Terence Moore/Ronchetti Design; 56 tl and bl The Interior Archive/Mark Luscombe –Whyte/Jose de Yturbe; 56-57 Dennis Gilbert/VIEW; 58 t Richard Powers/Warren & Mahoney/New Zealand; 58 b Iain Kemp/Taylor Howes Designs; 59 t and bl Jean-Luc Laloux/Tenarquitectos; 59 br Phil Aynsley Photography; 60-61 Garden Picture Library/Steven Wooster; 62-65 Richard Powers/Marmol Radziner/Carole Katelman; 66-69 Garden Picture Library/Ron Sutherland; 70 tl Clive Nichols/Scott Stover, France; 70 tr Andreas von Einsiedel; 70 bl Jean-Luc Laloux; 70 br Jean-Luc Laloux/Axell Vervoordt; 71 b The Interior Archive/Christopher Simon Sykes; 71 t Jean-Francois Jaussaud/Luxproductions; 72-73 Garden Exposures; 73 b Garden Exposures/Andrea Jones/Topher Delaney; 74-75 Nicola Browne/Piet Boon/Piet Oudolf; 76 tl The Interior Archive/Mark Luscombe-Whyte; 76 tr The Interior Archive/Christopher Simon Sykes; 76 bl Arcaid/Richard Waite; 77 t Garden Exposures/Andrea Jones/Topher Delaney; 77 cl The Interior Archive/Mark Lucsombe-Whyte/Antti Louag; 77 bl Paul Massey/Mainstream Images; 77 br Peter Glass and Associates, Landscape Architects and Pool Designers, Sydney Australia. www.peterglass.com.au; 78 Jean-Francois Jaussaud/Luxproductions; 79 Andrew Wood/Gandia Blasco/Ramon Esteve; 80-81 Andreas von Einsiedel; 82-83 Jean-Luc Laloux; 84-85 Ray Main/Michaelis Boyd Associates; 86-87 Ray Main; 87 inset l Gloster; 87 inset c Ray Main/Michaelis Boyd Associates; 87 inset r Ray Main/Georg Riedel/Gunther Weidner ; 88 Andrew Wood/Karim El Achak Architect; 90 l Andreas von Einsiedel; 90 r Jean-Luc Laloux/Howland; 91 tl Andreas von Einsiedel; 91 tr The Interior Archive/Fritz von der Schulenburg/Chambers; 91 b Jean-Francois Jaussaud/Luxproductions; 92 tl Jean-Luc Laloux; 92 bl Jean-Francois Jaussaud/Luxproductions; 92-93 Jean-Luc Laloux/Bruno Erpicum; 94-95 Jean-Luc Laloux/Bruno Erpicum; 96 t Arcaid/Nicholas Kane/Belsize Architects; 96 b David Hallam Ltd; 97 tr Jean-Francois Jaussaud/Luxproductions; 97 br Jean-Francois Jaussaud/Luxproductions; 97 l Jean-Luc Laloux/Bernardo Gomez/Tenarquitectos; 98-101 Ray Main/Michaelis Boyd Associates; 102 bl Arcaid/Jeremy Cockayne/Paxton Locher Architects; 102 br Endless Pools; 102 tl and tr Kissel; 102 cr Poolside Magazine/Patrick Redmond/Baden Pools; 103 l and r Kissel; 104-107 Ray Main/Mainstream Images; 108 Anson Smart – Photographer; 110 Taylor Howes Design/Iain Kemp; 111 tl The Interior Archive/Mark Luscombe-Whyte/Fabrizio Bizzari & Alessandra Lippini; 111 tr The Interior Archive/Fritz von der Schulenburg/Child & Co.; 111 ac The Interior Archive/Fritz von der Schulenburg; 111 b Andreas von Einsiedel; 112-113 Clive Frost/Rainbow Pools; 114 Fuchs baut Garten/Klas Stover; 115 t and b Biotop www.swimming-teich.com; 116-117 Fuchs baut Garten/Klas Stover; 118 t Arcaid/Alan Weintraub/Bart Prince; 118 b Trevor Mein/Wood Marsh Architects; 119 Arcaid/Alan Weintraub/Lautner Associates; 120-123 Ray Main/Georg Riedel/Gunther Weidner; 124 tl Terence Moore/Ronchetti; 124 tr The Interior Archive/Fritz von der Schulenburg; 124 bl Phil Aynsley Photography; 124 br The Interior Archive/Mark Luscombe-Whyte/Eli Moujal; 125 Freedom Pools Central Coast/Australia; 125 bl Poolside Magazine/Tim Turner/Neptune Pools and Seidler Homes; 125 br Clive Nichols/Cesar Manrique; 126-127 Andrew Wood/Seth Stein; 128-131 Ray Main; 131 inset l Phil Aynsley Photography; 131 inset c Fuchs baut Garten/Klas Stover; 131 inset r Ray Main/Munkenbeck and Marshall; 132 Rainbow Pools; 133 tl Nicola Browne/Oscar Tusquets; 133 b Rainbow Pools; 133 tr Richard Powers/Design King, Sydney; 134 Jean-Francois Jaussaud/Luxproductions; 135 Vinny Lee; 136 tl Terence Moore/Ronchetti; 136 tr The Interior Archive/Mark Luscombe-Whyte/Manolo Meste; 136 b Garden Exposures/Andrea Jones; 137 The Interior Archive/ Mark Luscombe-Whyte/Antii Louag; 138 tl Phil Aynsley Photography; 138 tr Arcaid/John Edward Linden/John Newton; 138 bl Nicola Browne/Isabelle Greene; 138 br Andrew Wood/Johann Slee; 139 t Neptune Pools; 139 b The Interior Archive/Simon Upton; 140 t Andreas von Einsiedel; 140 Nicola Browne; 141 t Jean-Francois Jaussaud/Luxproductions; 141 b Arcaid/Richard Bryant/Seth Stein Architects; 142 tl The Interior Archive/Mark Luscombe-Whyte/Jose de Yturbe; 142 tr David Hallam Ltd; 142 b Dennis Gilbert/VIEW; 143 Andrew Wood/Johann Slee; 144 l The Interior Archive/Fritz von der Schulenburg/John Stefanidis; 144 r David Hallam Ltd; 145 Richard Glover/VIEW; 146 Andreas von Einsiedel; 147 t Christian Michel/VIEW; 147 br Anson Smart – Photographer; 147 bl Andreas von Einsiedel; 148 t The Interior Archive/Helen Fickling/Lari Rosenberg; 148 b Phil Aynsley Photography; 149 tl Nicola Browne/Thomas Church; 149 tr The Interior Archive/Mark Luscombe-Whyte/Jose de Yturbe; 149 bl Johann Slee; 149 br The Interior Archive/Helen Fickling/Karel Nel; 150 t Serge Brison; 150 b Fuchs baut Garten/Klas Stover; 151 tl Clive Nichols/Cesar Manrique; 151 tr The Interior Archive/Mark Lucsombe-Whyte/© 2005 Barragan Foundation, Birsfelden, Switzerland / ProLitteris, Zürich, Switzerland for the entire work of Luis Barragán; 151 Tim Brotherton; 152 l and r Ray Main/Powell Tuck Associates/Deepwater; 153 Ray Main/ Ray Main/Georg Riedel/Gunther Weidner; 154 Tim Brotherton; 155 Jean-Francois Jaussaud/Luxproductions; 156 tl Andreas von Einsiedel; 156 tr SCDA Architects/Albert Lim; 156 bl Phil Aynsley Photography; 156 Dennis Gilbert/VIEW; 157 cr Nicola Browne/Steve Martino; 157 bt Poolside Magazine/Tim Turner/Fiberstars; 158 l Dennis Gilbert/VEIW/Kallosturin Associates; 158 r Serge Brison; 159 t Ray Main/Georg Riedel/Gunther Weidner; 159 b Ray Main/Michaelis Boyd Associates; 160 l The Interior Archive/Simon Upton/John Stedila; 160 r The Interior Archive/Simon Upton/Anthony Collett; 161 t Simon Upton/Architect Gilles Pellerin's house in Cannes; 161 b Arcaid/Alan Weintraub/Daniel Piechota; 162 l Jean-Luc Laloux/Bruno Erpicum; 162 cr Sarkis Boyadjian/Bobby Desai; 162 tr The Interior Archive/Christopher Simon Sykes/Vivian Leone; 163 Jean-Luc Laloux/Pascal Vanderkelen; 164 t Dedon/Christophe Dugied, Paris; 164 bl Serge Brison; 164 br Terence Moore; 165 bl Marls & Spencer; 165 cr Gloster; 165 br Jean-Francois Jaussaud/Luxproductions; 166 l Gloster; 166 r Conmoto; 167 t Marks & Spencer; 167 b Arcaid/Alberto Piovano/Vincent van Duysen; 168 t Peter Cook/VIEW/Mclean Quinlan Arhitects; 168 b Andreas von Einsiedel; 169 tl Dennis Gilbert/VIEW; 169 tr Dedon/Christophe Dugied, Paris; 169 cl Jean-Luc Laloux/Bruno Stoppa; 169 bl Aaron Pocock; 170 l Hufton & Crow/VIEW; 170 r Jean-Francois Jaussaud/Luxproductions; 171 Christian Michel/VIEW; 172 t Anson Smart – Photographer; 172 bl Andrew Wood/Johann Slee; 172 br Andreas von Einsiedel; 173 Serge Brison; 174-175 Tim Brotherton; 175 br Arcaid/Alan Weintraub/John Lautner; 176 t Ray Main/Georg Riedel/Gunther Weidner; 176 bl Fuchs baut Garten/Klas Stover; 176 br Anson Smart – Photographer; 177 t Jean-Luc Laloux/Alberto Kalach; 177 b Kissel; 178 tl David Hallam Ltd; 178 tr A&T Europe/Golden Coast; 178 b Peter Cook/VIEW/Mclean Quinlan Architects; 179 Ray Main/Munkenbeck and Marshall; 180 t and b David Hallam Ltd; 181 tl , tr and br David Hallam Ltd; 181 bl Kissel; 183 Dennis Gilbert/VIEW.

AUTHOR'S ACKNOWLEDGMENTS

Many thanks to Jacqui, Kate, Sian, Emily and Ashley, who made this book possible, and to all the architects, designers and photographers who supplied information and images; also to Ray who brought his weather wand with him.

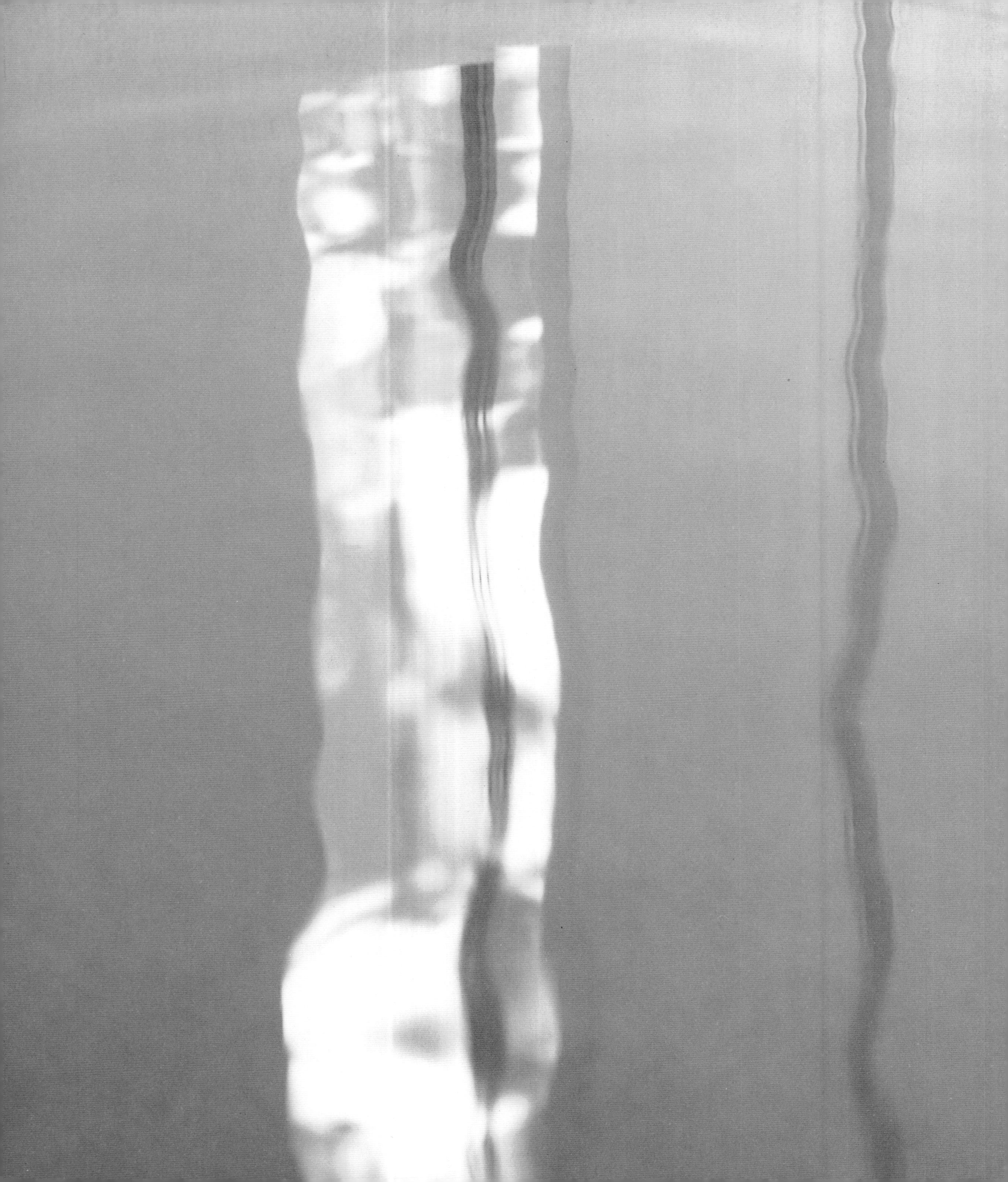